GREYSCALE
BIN TRAVELER FORM

Cut By: Mohit J Malio   Qty: 37   Date: 02/05/20

Scanned By: _____ Qty: _____ Date: _____

Scanned Batch ID's: _____

Notes / Exception:

AMERICAN HERITAGE

December 1961 · Volume XIII, Number 1

© 1961 by American Heritage Publishing Co., Inc. All rights reserved under Berne and Pan-American Copyright Conventions. Reproduction in whole or in part of any article without permission is prohibited. U.S. copyright is not claimed for color plates on pages 8–11, 18–21, 24–29, 36, 49–51, 53–55, 62–64, 66–67, and 71.

AMERICAN WINTER SPORTS
TROUT FISHING "ON CHATEAUGAY LAKE"

The trout were magnificent, and the winter solitude of the remote Adirondack lakes a joy to the sportsman before the tourist discovered them. This popular 1856 Currier & Ives print of ice fishing on Chateaugay Lake in New York was made from a painting by the greatest sporting artist of that day, Arthur Fitzwilliam Tait.

AMERICAN HERITAGE

The Magazine of History

PUBLISHER
James Parton
EDITORIAL DIRECTOR
Joseph J. Thorndike, Jr.
SENIOR EDITOR
Bruce Catton
EDITOR
Oliver Jensen
MANAGING EDITOR
Eric Larrabee
ASSOCIATE EDITORS
Richard M. Ketchum
Joan Paterson Mills
Robert L. Reynolds
ASSISTANT EDITORS
Robert Cowley, Meryle Evans
Stephen W. Sears
CONTRIBUTING EDITOR
Margery Darrell
LIBRARIAN
Caroline Backlund
COPY EDITOR
Beverly Hill
ASSISTANT: Suzanne Adessa

SENIOR ART DIRECTOR
Irwin Glusker
ART DIRECTOR
Murray Belsky
STAFF PHOTOGRAPHER: Herbert Loebel

ADVISORY BOARD
Allan Nevins, *Chairman*
Ray A. Billington   Alvin M. Josephy, Jr.
Carl Carmer   Richard P. McCormick
Albert B. Corey   Harry Shaw Newman
Christopher Crittenden   Howard H. Peckham
Marshall B. Davidson   S. K. Stevens
Louis C. Jones   Arthur M. Schlesinger, Sr.

AMERICAN HERITAGE is published every two months by American Heritage Publishing Co., Inc., 551 Fifth Avenue, New York 17, N.Y. Correspondence about subscriptions should be addressed to: American Heritage Subscription Office, 383 West Center Street, Marion, Ohio. Single Copies: $3.95. Annual Subscriptions: $15.00 in U.S. & Canada; $16.00 elsewhere.

An annual Index of AMERICAN HERITAGE is published every February, priced at $1.00. A Cumulative Index of Volumes VI–X is available at $3.00.

AMERICAN HERITAGE will consider but assumes no responsibility for unsolicited material. Title registered U.S. Patent Office. Second class postage paid at New York, N.Y.

Sponsored by
American Association for State & Local History · Society of American Historians

CONTENTS   December 1961 · Volume XIII, Number 1

BRYAN: *The Progressives, Part I,* by John A. Garraty	4
AMERICAN HERITAGE BOOK SELECTION	
THE PARSON AND THE BLUESTOCKING *by Martha Bacon*	12
FACES FROM THE PAST—V *by Richard M. Ketchum*	16
THE OLD SHOWMAN'S LAST TRIUMPH *by Eric Larrabee*	18
THE WATER WAR *by Remi Nadeau*	30
THE SUNNY MASTER OF SUNNYSIDE *by Curtis Dahl*	36
JACK JOUETT'S RIDE *by Virginius Dabney*	56
CAPTAIN COOK'S AMERICAN *by E. M. Halliday*	60
THE GREAT DECEPTION *by Moshe Decter*	73
(AMERICA AND RUSSIA: PART XI)	
"I KNEEL ONLY TO GOD AND WOMAN" *by Horace Knowles*	94
READING, WRITING, AND HISTORY *by Bruce Catton*	116
A CIVIL WAR PROPOSAL	120

COVER: Early in the 1770's, after his return from the first of three momentous voyages to the Pacific, Captain James Cook of the Royal Navy sat for the portraitist Nathaniel Dance. A Yorkshire farmboy who became one of the greatest maritime explorers of all time, Cook charted more miles of unknown coastline than any Englishman before him, claimed Australia and New Zealand for the Crown, and discovered the island chain that would one day be our fiftieth state, Hawaii. The story of Cook's last, tragic voyage and of John Ledyard, the Yankee visionary who accompanied him, is told in E. M. Halliday's "Captain Cook's American" (page 60). Dance's portrait of Cook now hangs in the National Maritime Museum at Greenwich, England. *Back Cover:* A flowery Currier & Ives motto, suitable for framing in a nineteenth-century parlor, is reproduced through the courtesy of the Museum of the City of New York.

3

BROWN BROTHERS

BRYAN:

exhibit one in a gallery of men who fought the good fight in vain

Americans are a proud, ambitious, and hopeful people; they are easily riled when life does not measure up to their expectations, and quick to express their displeasure. Only one "era of good feelings" is recorded in our history; it was short, merely superficially calm, and quickly followed by the broils and battles of the Age of Jackson. On the other hand, fundamental conflicts of interest and opinion among Americans have been extremely rare. Our Constitution, for example, has been amended only a dozen times since the Bill of Rights was added nearly two hundred years ago; it is not basically different today from what it was then.

This combination of over-all placidity and local tumult is understandable. America has been generally receptive to new ideas, but has not tended to swallow

Bryan on the sawdust trail: In an age before the microphone, his stentorian voice could reach tens of thousands unassisted.

THE PROGRESSIVES: Part I

By JOHN A. GARRATY

them whole. Reformers who want to make basic changes seldom get far in our system; although their reforms are often achieved, they themselves seldom achieve power. Traditionally this "law" of American politics has been explained by the tendency of the major parties to make concessions to radical ideas as soon as they show signs of becoming popular, and by the generally happy and prosperous condition of the American people, which has predisposed them toward moderation and gradualism. I would like to suggest, without fundamentally questioning that view, that reformers also defeat themselves, not through the ends they cherish but by the means they choose.

This article and two that will follow will try to demonstrate this proposition by examining the careers of three reformers of the Progressive Era, that period from the turn of the century to World War I when America was adjusting to its rapid emergence as a great industrial nation. Our subjects are William Jennings Bryan, a Democrat; George W. Perkins, one of Theodore Roosevelt's "Bull Moosers"; and Robert M. La Follette, until the tag end of his long career always a Republican. Despite the diversity of their politics all three considered themselves "progressives," and have been accepted as such by historians. All were "good" men, utterly incorruptible, who devoted their lives to fruitful public service. All accomplished a great deal. But all, in the end, failed to achieve their chief objectives. What went right? What went wrong?

That is our story. —J. A. G.

Harper's Weekly, January 18, 1908

"I Feel the Delusion Coming on Again."

His public life spanned a half century. Three times his hand reached for the nation's highest office. But at the end he was a relic of the past, an object of ridicule or pity

ROLLIN KIRBY, NEW YORK *World*, MAY 19, 1925; CULVER PICTURE

Gathering Data for the Tennessee Trial

"The President of the United States may be an ass," wrote H. L. Mencken during the reign of Calvin Coolidge, "but he at least doesn't believe that the earth is square, and that witches should be put to death, and that Jonah swallowed the whale." The man to whom the vitriolic Mencken was comparing President Coolidge was William Jennings Bryan of Nebraska, one of the dominant figures in the Progressive movement. According to Mencken, Bryan was a "peasant," a "zany without sense or dignity," a "poor clod," and, in addition, an utter fraud. "If the fellow was sincere, then so was P. T. Barnum," he sneered.

It was certainly easy enough, and tempting, for sophisticates to come to the conclusion that Bryan was a buffoon and a fake. His undignified association in his declining years with the promotion of Florida real estate and his naïve and bigoted religious views, so pitilessly exposed by Clarence Darrow during the famous "Monkey Trial" in Dayton, Tennessee, lent substance to the Mencken view of his character. So did Bryan's smug refusal, while Secretary of State under Woodrow Wilson, to serve alcoholic beverages at Department receptions and dinners because of his personal disapproval of drinking, and his objection to the appointment of ex-President Charles W. Eliot of Harvard as Ambassador to China on the ground that Eliot was a Unitarian, and therefore not a real Christian. "The new Chinese civilization," said Bryan, "was founded upon the Christian movement." Eliot's appointment might undermine the work of generations of pious missionaries, he implied. Bryan's unabashed partisanship—he talked frankly after Wilson's election of filling government positions with "deserving Democrats"—did not seem to jibe with his pretensions as a reformer. And his oratorical style, magnificent but generally more emotional than logical, was disappointing to thinking people. John Hay called him a "Baby Demosthenes" and David Houston, one of his colleagues in Wilson's Cabinet, stated that "one could drive a prairie schooner through any part of his argument and never scrape against a fact." Being largely a creature of impulse, Bryan was, Houston added, "constantly on the alert to get something which has been represented to him as a fact to support or sustain his impulses."

But these flaws and blind spots were not fundamental weaknesses; they should never be allowed to overshadow Bryan's long years of devoted service to the cause of reform. If there were large areas about which he knew almost nothing, there were others where he was alert, sensible, and well-informed; certainly he was not a stupid man, nor was he easily duped or misled. Although a professional politician, as his remark about "deserving Democrats" makes clear, he was utterly honest personally and devoted to the cause of the people, as he understood it.

He was perfectly attuned to the needs and aspirations of rural America. In the early nineties he was in the forefront of the fight against high tariffs on manufactured goods. Later in the decade he battled for currency reform. At the turn of the century he was leading the assault against imperialism. During Theodore Roosevelt's primacy he was often far ahead of the intrepid Teddy, advocating a federal income tax, the eight-hour day, the control of monopoly and the strict regulation of public utilities, woman suffrage, and a large number of other startling innovations. Under

Wilson he played a major part in marshaling support in Congress for the Federal Reserve Act and other New Freedom measures. Whatever his limitations, his faults, or his motives, few public men of his era left records as consistently "progressive" as Bryan's.

For years he led the Democratic party without the advantage of holding office. Three times he was a presidential candidate; although never elected, he commanded the unswerving loyalty of millions of his fellow citizens for nearly thirty years. He depended more on his intuition than on careful analysis in forming his opinions, but his intuition was usually sound; he was more a man of heart than of brain, but his heart was great.

Bryan was known as the Great Commoner, and the title was apt. He was a man of the people in origin and by instinct. He was typical of his age in rendering great respect to public opinion, whether it was informed or not. To Bryan the voice of the people was truly the voice of God. "I don't know anything about free silver," he announced while running for Congress early in the nineties. "The people of Nebraska are for free silver and I am for free silver. I will look up the arguments later." (It should be added that he did indeed "look up the arguments later." Less than a year after making this promise he arose in the House to deliver without notes a brilliant three-hour speech on the money question, a speech of great emotional power, but also fact-laden, sensible, and full of shrewd political arguments. When he sat down, the cheers rang out from both sides of the aisle.)

Bryan was born in Salem, Illinois, in 1860, a child of the great Middle West. Growing up in the heart of the valley of democracy, he absorbed its spirit and its sense of protest from his earliest years. After being graduated from Illinois College in 1881, he studied law in Chicago and for a time practiced his profession in Jacksonville, Illinois. But in 1887, stimulated by a talk with a law-school classmate from that city, he moved west to Lincoln, Nebraska. He quickly made his way in this new locale. Within a year he was active in the local Democratic organization, and in 1890, a month before his thirtieth birthday, he won his party's nomination for congressman.

Nebraska was traditionally a Republican state, its loyalty to the party of Lincoln forged in the heat of the Civil War. But by 1890 tradition was rapidly losing its hold on voters all over the Middle West. For the farmers of the American heartland were in deep trouble, and the Republican party seemed unwilling to do much to help them.

Tumultuous social and economic changes shaped the nation in the years after Appomattox. Within a single generation the United States was transformed from what was essentially a land of farmers into a modern industrial society, and in the process the Middle West was caught in a relentless economic vise. During the flush times of the sixties, when the Union Army was buying enormous amounts of food and fodder, and foreign demand was unusually high, the farmers of the region had gone into debt in order to buy more land and machinery. In the seventies and eighties, however, agricultural prices, especially those of such major staple crops as wheat and cotton, fell steeply. Wheat, which had sold as high as $2.50 a bushel in wartime, was down to fifty cents by the early nineties.

The impact of this economic decline was intensified by the changing social status of the farmer. Agriculture was losing its predominant place in American life. In the days of the Founding Fathers, about ninety per cent of the population was engaged in working the soil, and the farmer was everywhere portrayed as the symbol of American self-reliance and civic virtue. "Those who labor in the earth," Jefferson said, "are the chosen people of God." But as the factory began to outstrip the farm, the farmer lost much of his standing. While the old symbol remained—it was especially in evidence around election time—a new and disturbing image of the farmer as a hick, a rube, a hayseed— a comic mixture of cocky ignorance, shrewd self-interest, and monumental provincialism—began to challenge it.

Naturally the farmers resented their loss of both income and prestige, but there was little they could do about either. Price declines were largely a response to worldwide overproduction, resulting from improvements in transportation and the opening up of new farmlands in Australia, Argentina, Canada, Russia, and elsewhere. Nor did the farmers, who desired manufactured goods as much as everyone else, really want to reverse the trend that was making them a minority group in a great industrial nation. But as they cast about for some way out of their plight, they were profoundly disturbed by certain results of the new development which did seem amenable to reform.

Industrial growth meant the mushrooming of great cities. These gave birth to noxious slums where every kind of vice flourished, where corrupt political organizations like the venal Tweed Ring in New York were forged, and where radical political concepts like socialism and anarchism sought to undermine "the American way of life." In the words of Jefferson, the farmers' hero, cities were "ulcers on the body politic."

"BLOWING" HIMSELF AROUND THE COUNTRY.

This Puck *cartoon of 1896 represents the eastern, Republican view of Bryan's audience as a rabble of farmers and yokels to whom his principal campaign plank, the free coinage of silver at a ratio of 16 to 1 with gold, meant easy money—and, Republicans earnestly believed, the utter ruination of the economy.*

Giant industries also attracted hordes of immigrants; these seemed to threaten the Middle West both by their mere numbers and by their "un-American" customs and points of view. Could the American melting pot absorb such strange ingredients without losing much of its own character?

Furthermore, to the citizens of Nebraska and other agricultural states, the new industrial barons appeared bent on making vassals of every farmer in America. The evidence seemed overwhelming: Huge impersonal corporations had neither souls nor consciences; profit was their god, materialism their only creed. The "interests," a tiny group of powerful tycoons in great eastern centers like Boston, New York, and Philadelphia, were out to enslave the rest of the country. Farmers worked and sweated only to see the "interests" make off with most of the fruit of their toil. Too many useless middlemen grew fat off the mere "handling" of wheat and cotton. Monopolistic railroads overcharged for carrying crops to market, unscrupulous operators of grain elevators falsely downgraded prime crops and charged exorbitant fees. Cynical speculators drove the price of staples up and down, sometimes making and losing millions in a matter of minutes, without the slightest regard for the effect of their operations on the producers whose sweat made their deadly game possible.

Conspiring with bankers and mortgage holders, all these groups combined to dictate the federal government's money policy. Population and production were surging forward; more money was needed simply to keep up with economic growth. Yet the government was deliberately cutting down on the amount of money in circulation by retiring Civil War greenbacks. On debt-ridden farmers plagued by overproduction, the effect of this deflation was catastrophic. Or so it seemed from the perspective of rural America.

While undoubtedly exaggerated, this indictment of the "interests" was taken as gospel throughout large sectors of the South and West. As a result, demands for "reform" quickly arose. The leading reformers were for the most part sincere, but few of them were entirely altruistic and many were decidedly eccentric. Participating in the movement for a variety of motives but without coming to grips with the main problem of American agriculture—overproduction—were coarse demagogues like Senator "Pitchfork Ben" Tillman of South Carolina, and unwashed characters like the wise-cracking congressman from Kansas, "Sockless Jerry" Simpson. There were professional orators like the angry Mary Ellen Lease (her detractors called her "Mary Yellin'"), and homespun economic theorists like "Coin" Harvey and "General" Jacob Coxey, who believed so strongly in paper money that he named his son Legal Tender. The excesses of such people frightened off many Americans who might otherwise have lent a sympathetic ear to the farmers' complaints; others who might have been friendly observed the antics of the reformers with contempt and wrote off the whole movement as a joke.

Since neither of the major parties espoused the farmers' cause wholeheartedly, much of the protest found its way into various third-party organizations. At first, discontented elements concentrated on opposing the government's policy of retiring the paper money put in circulation during the Civil War. To save these greenbacks from extinction a Greenback (later Greenback-Labor) party sprang up. In 1878 its candidates polled a million votes, but decline followed as currency reformers turned to other methods of inflation.

Meanwhile the Patrons of Husbandry, better known as the Grange, originally a social organization for farm families, had begun to agitate in local politics against the middlemen who were draining off such a large percentage of the farmers' profits. In the seventies the Grangers became a power in the Middle West; in state after state they obtained the passage of laws setting maximum rates for railroads and prohibiting various forms of discrimination. The operations of grain elevators were also subjected to state regulation by "Granger Laws" in states such as Illinois, Iowa, Wisconsin, and Minnesota. The Grange abandoned political activity in the eighties, but other farm organizations quickly took its place. These coalesced first into the Northern Alliance and the Southern Alliance, and around 1890 the two Alliances joined with one another to become the Populist party.

Although William Jennings Bryan was a Democrat, he had grown up amid the agitations of the Granger movement. His father had even run for Congress in the seventies with Greenback party support. The aspirations and the general point of view of the midwestern farmers were young Bryan's own. Public men, he admitted late in life to the journalist Mark Sullivan, are "the creatures of their age. . . . I lived in the very center of the country out of which the reforms grew, and was quite naturally drawn to the people's side."

And they to his, one must add. Discontented farmers in his district were on the lookout for men who understood them and their problems. In 1888 the Republicans had carried the seat by 3,000 votes; now, in 1890, Bryan swept in with a lead of 6,713.

Bryan made an excellent record in his first Congress. He was a hardworking member, studying the technicalities of the tariff question for months before making his first important speech. But he saw that the tariff was rapidly being replaced by the money question as the crucial issue of the day. When he yielded the floor after completing his tariff speech, he collared a young Texas congressman named Joseph W. Bailey, who posed as a financial expert. Sitting on a sofa in the rear of the House chamber, he quizzed Bailey about the problem of falling prices. Bailey told him the tariff had little or no effect on the plight of the farmer; the whole difficulty arose from "an appreciation in value of gold." Interested, Bryan demanded a list of books on the subject and was soon deep in a study of the money question.

To a man like Bryan, studying the money question meant searching for some means of checking the de-

COLLECTION OF J. DOYLE DE WITT

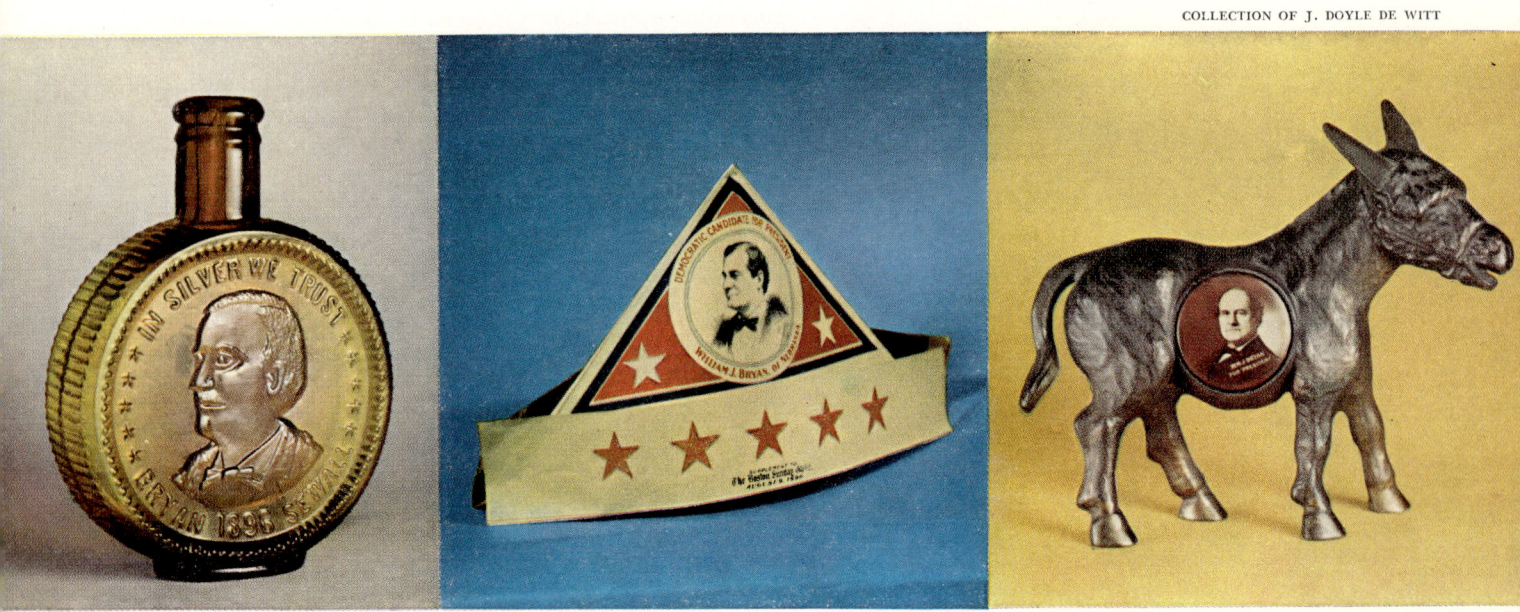

A glass flask, its barrel in the shape of a silver dollar, is a souvenir of the 1896 election, as is the paper hat. Small donkeys were popular among Bryan men in 1900. That year the Nebraskan shared billing on

flationary trend that was so injurious to his farmer constituents. He quickly discovered that most farm-belt financial authorities felt this could best be done by providing for the free coinage of silver. In 1873 the United States had gone on the gold standard, which meant that only gold was accepted for coinage at the mint. By going back to bimetallism, the amount of bullion being coined would be increased, and if the favorable ratio of sixteen to one between silver and gold were established, the production of silver for coinage would be greatly stimulated.

To press for the free coinage of silver at a ratio of sixteen to one with gold seemed less radical or dangerous than to demand direct inflation of the currency through the printing of greenbacks. Silver, after all, was a precious metal; coining it could not possibly lead to the sort of "runaway" inflation that had helped ruin the South during the Civil War. Debtors and other friends of inflation could also count on the powerful support of silver-mine interests. The free-coinage issue thus had a powerful political appeal. Despite the opposition of most conservative businessmen, the silverites were able, in 1878 and again in 1890, to obtain legislation providing for the coinage of *some* silver, although not enough to check the downward trend of prices.

Within a month after his tariff speech Bryan was calling for free coinage, and he stressed the issue in his successful campaign for re-election in 1892. But the new President, Democrat Grover Cleveland, was an ardent gold-standard man, and when a severe depression struck the country early in 1893, he demanded that the Silver Purchase Act of 1890, which had raised the specter of inflation in the minds of many businessmen, be repealed by Congress at once. In this way he committed his party to the resumption of the single gold standard.

Bryan refused to go along with this policy. Threatening to "serve my country and my God under some other name" than "Democrat" unless the Administration changed its mind, he resisted the repeal of the silver act in a brilliant extemporaneous speech. Cleveland carried the day for repeal, but Bryan emerged as a potential leader of the silver wing of the Democrats.

In 1894 he sought a wider influence by running for the United States Senate. In those days senators were still chosen by the state legislatures; to be elected Bryan would need the support of Nebraska's Populists as well as of his own party. He worked hard for fusion, but Populist support was not forthcoming. Though the Democrats backed Populist candidate Silas A. Holcomb for the governorship, the Populists refused to reciprocate and ran their own man for the Senate seat. The Republican candidate therefore won easily.

At this stage the Populists were trying hard to become a truly national party. Their program, besides demanding the free coinage of silver and various land reforms desired by farmers, called for government ownership of railroads, a graduated income tax, the direct election of U.S. senators, the eight-hour day, and a number of additional reforms designed to appeal to eastern workingmen and other dissatisfied groups. As early as 1892 their presidential candidate, James B. Weaver, had polled over a million votes; in 1894 the party won six seats in the Senate and seven in the House of Representatives. At least in Nebraska, the Populists were not yet ready to merge with the "conservative" Democratic organization.

CONTINUED ON PAGE 108

buttons with his running mate, whose grandson and namesake, now Ambassador to the United Nations, has had his picture on some buttons too. The plate, pins, and watch fobs date from Bryan's last race, in 1908.

The spinster thought she'd been proposed to; the young minister thought not. Their courtship and quarrel rocked devout New Haven

The Parson and the Bluestocking

By MARTHA BACON

AMERICAN HERITAGE BOOK SELECTION

Delia Bacon

When we scan the newspapers of New England for the year 1847 we are inclined to marvel at what failed to constitute a scandal in those pre-atomic times. Inserted among notices of mortgage sales and advertisements for elixirs guaranteed to cure everything from the croup to a dropped womb, we come upon such stirring accounts as that of Eliza McCormick, a servant girl who masqueraded as a bank clerk on her Sundays off and attempted the seduction of several other servant girls. "She is thought to be," remarked the journalist who covered the story, "the same person who figured at Galt a short time since under the disguise of a sick sailor." Eliza figured no further in the public press that spring, although a number of eccentric cases succeeded her. Two fine baby boys in an expensive lying-in establishment were mixed up—so hopelessly that their distracted mothers were urged simply to pick a child and go home, since there was no possible way of deciding which infant was whose. A man in Florida paid out a grudge by capturing the object of his ill will, tying him to an alligator, and then setting fire to the alligator, with the unhappiest consequences for both man and beast. Princess Demidoff, dressed in a man's clothes, horsewhipped her husband's mistress. And a member of a highly respected New England family joined an Arab tribe and became notable for his war chant, "Old Hundred," which he rendered with an invincible Yankee twang as he galloped with his Bedouins into battle.

Not one of these items, newsworthy as they may now seem to us, merited more than two inches of space in any Connecticut paper. The scandal of the year was the affair of Miss Delia Bacon and the Reverend Alexander MacWhorter.

At the time of this tribulation Delia Bacon had not yet become famous as one of the chief supporters of the theory that William Shakespeare was merely a pseudonym for Sir Francis Bacon, Sir Walter Raleigh, and others. A highbred bluestocking of thirty-five, in 1845 she had met Alexander MacWhorter, a twenty-three-year-old clergyman, in the New Haven boardinghouse where they were both living; and in spite of the unfavorable disparity in their ages they fell in love, or so Miss Bacon ultimately asserted. MacWhorter for his part swore to the contrary. The consequences of their encounter turned out to be something that was bigger than both of them. Their lovers' quarrel was absorbed into a wrangle for authority, intemperate and unseemly, between the parochial clergy of the city of New Haven and the faculty of the Yale Divinity School. The Congregational Church was touched on the quick; for MacWhorter was the protégé of Nathaniel William Taylor, professor of didactic theology at Yale and one of the most powerful men in Connecticut. Delia, on

12

the other hand, was not only a celebrated *femme savante* but the sister of Taylor's close friend, Leonard Bacon, pastor of the First Church of Christ (or Center Church), the fountainhead of Connecticut Calvinism and chief shrine of the Establishment in the commonwealth.

New Haven in the forties was a gay city and at that time one of the handsomest towns in New England. In defiance perhaps of its Cromwellian beginnings (it had been a refuge for regicides during the Restoration) and the monastic pattern of its university, it was proud of its newly formed Beethoven Society, its good taverns, and the beauty and wit of its women. Its chief commodity, however, was the Congregational clergy. Ministers served as the backbone of its society, its principal export and finest ornament.

In addition to its ghostly powers the priest caste of New Haven exercised considerable temporal ones, inasmuch as the clergy owned a large proportion of the land of the commonwealth. Churchmen were thus able to perform with scarifying audacity the roles of both yogi and commissar, governing a demesne whose limits stretched from the cradle to well beyond the grave. Of this the elders whose duty it was to license young divines were keenly aware. The church required that the character of any minister be unimpeachable. His scholarship, his morals, and his orthodoxy underwent the severest scrutiny before the Congregational hobbledehoy ascended the pulpit. Here and there a misfit occurred, such as the Reverend Azel Backus, who "could not keep his drolleries out of the pulpit" and "lived a life of questionable propriety" while the souls under his care tittered their way to perdition; but he seems to have been as odd as an owl trooping among chickens. Clergymen in general avoided levity, lived by the book, mastered the Greek, Latin, and Hebrew tongues, married blameless behavior to a set of stern beliefs, and graced it all with the uses and accomplishments of a gentleman. Such a man was Nathaniel Taylor, the Rhadamanthus of Delia Bacon's ordeal, and such a man was his antagonist, Leonard Bacon.

A hundred years earlier New Haven had had no God but Yahweh, and Jonathan Edwards was his prophet. The brimstone perorations that sizzled from New England pulpits had caused women to faint and strong men to shudder in their beds at the mere recollection. But by 1845 a younger and more impressionable generation was bringing a Byronic sensibility to the exacerbated conscience of Calvinism. (Byron seems to have had great charm for the adherents of this savage creed: there was an unmistakable allure in one so militantly, not to say joyously, damned.)

The Old Calvinists were poulticing the bruises received from the Unitarians and the heretical Henry Ward Beecher, and though Nathaniel Taylor preached on infant damnation, one senses that he was not wholly for it. He had even made a strong case for free will in his controversy with Bennet Tyler twenty years previously. But now from "bawling and quarreling about the Trinity" the parsons and their parishioners had fallen victim to a fit of salvation by works, while the salvation-through-grace-alone faction smouldered in the ascendant within the university, free will notwithstanding. But the rank-and-file preacher continued to boom with reforming zeal, replacing the totemic deity with something that closely resembled a kindly social worker. Antislavery was a hotter issue than antinomianism. Yahweh suffered further from the rising cluster of scientists who ignored him and from women—intellectual women, such women as Lyman Beecher's wives and daughters—who simply regarded him as a frightful mistake. The doctrinaire Calvinists had heard themselves roundly refuted by Delia Bacon's mentor, Catharine Beecher, in 1836. Delia's assault upon MacWhorter took on the character of a thumping blow delivered at the infallibility of the Establishment, while his misuse of her confirmed the opposition in its suspicion that predestination made for poor preaching and worse practice. New Haven split over the matter like a melon in the sun.

In a city less remorselessly dynastic so ragged a rent in the garment of civic unity might not have shown so threadbare. But here, where Days married Shermans and Blakes married Thachers and Bacons married Wisners and the issue married their kith, while Taylors stood godparents to first-born Bacon babies, it was clear that death could not sunder the family party but, shockingly, Delia Bacon could.

The Bacon family were of the church churchly, and what they lacked in earthly goods they more than made up for in spiritual dignities and prestige. Leonard and Delia were the children of a missionary, David Bacon. Leonard had been born in that outpost of the Connecticut empire now known as Detroit. After Delia Salter's birth in 1811, David gave up his attempt to establish heaven on earth at Tallmadge, Ohio, and died heartbroken and debt-ridden, leaving his widow, Alice, with six children to rear. By various shifts she managed to educate all six. Leonard graduated from Yale at the age of eighteen, finished his theological studies at Andover, and entered on his pastorate at Center Church at the age of twenty-three. Delia, the youngest and most promising of the girls, early began to raise both hopes and apprehensions in the bosoms of her relatives. Clever, mercurial, and ambitious, she did not seem to know the meaning of the word moderation. When she caught the mumps, her sister Alice wrote to Leonard in real consternation that "Delia has a swelled face and has lost her reason." Delia's faculty for mislaying this article continued to be a source of genuine anxiety, but when in possession of her wits she showed herself industrious as a spider and ready to attack almost any difficulty if she glimpsed the possibility of a reward.

"Delia will do anything for money," wrote the hard-pressed Mrs. Bacon to her son in a letter that contains little else of an encouraging nature.

The little girl's natural liveliness was tempered with spasms of religious melancholy, common among children as measles or chicken pox in those days.

"Your sister has resisted the Holy Spirit and He has departed from me," she wrote at the age of ten to Leonard. "When I think of it I tremble. . . . oh, what will become of me when I leave this vain, transitory world and rise before my God in judgment? Cease not to pray for me. I have neglected the offers of salvation; I have despised my dear Redeemer but there is still mercy with Him who is able to save."

When Delia was about eleven, some friends of her mother's took her under their charge and enrolled her as a pupil at the female seminary in Hartford, recently established by Lyman Beecher's eldest daughter, Catharine. Here the volatile, bright-eyed youngster became a favorite not only with her teachers but with a fellow pupil, Catharine Beecher's droll, exquisite, and spirited little sister, Harriet.

Here is the child Delia as her twenty-two-year-old headmistress saw her: "An agreeable person, a pleasing and intelligent countenance, an eye of deep and earnest expression, a melodious voice, a fervid imagination and the embryo of rare gifts of eloquence." Miss Beecher's affection for the child did not blind her to Delia's flaws. She longed to excel, but more for the sake of applause than for any devotion to excellence. Love, recognition, and literary notoriety were far too dear to Delia in her teacher's estimation. She aimed for prizes, and when these eluded her, her disappointment was out of all proportion to the value that should have been placed on such trifles. Catharine describes her as a brilliant improviser but deficient when it came to organizing her material and getting it down according to the rules of unity, coherence, and emphasis. Worse, she was only intermittently pious, performing her religious duties sketchily enough to cause some concern as to the state of her soul. Catharine candidly admits that Delia was a handful. Fiercely competitive, she could not endure to see the work of others valued above her own, and when, as frequently happened, some other student gained the first place in class, her jealousy was so keen that her schoolfellows, who seem to have been a good-natured lot, were forced to forget their own triumphs in an effort to comfort and encourage her.

"Her keen sensibility," continues Catharine, "her transparency, sincerity and impulsiveness, the dangerous power of keen and witty expression . . . would make her an object of unjust depreciation. . . . The persons . . . who were the objects of her regard would almost immediately become enthusiastic admirers while those who in any way came into antagonism would be as decided in their dislike."

Only one likeness of Delia Bacon exists, a daguerreotype taken when she was in her forties. By all accounts it does not do her justice. The rich eye, the fine mobility of feature, the translucent complexion which though pale yet seemed to glow, are all absent. The woman whom Hawthorne described as "majestic . . . graceful," full of vivacity, dignity, and charm, has nothing in common with the strained and cynically smiling personage of the picture. It is a portrait of a sardonically tilted head, a warped mouth, two veined hands, a poke bonnet, and a cashmere shawl. Little is revealed of the creature who caught the attention of Emerson, Carlyle, and Hawthorne, and of whom Elizabeth Peabody wrote in a kind of rapture, as though there were something mesmeric in Delia.

"A beautiful being," declared Miss Peabody in a letter to Leonard Bacon after Delia's death. "A glorious and wonderful work of nature, most unhappily environed by uncongenial circumstances in many respects. Her entire unworldliness, her childlike character inspired me with a tenderness without bounds."

In the early 1800's New Haven's common was bordered by the Greek-revival Statehouse (center) and by three

But Miss Peabody strikes a dissonance in her paean. Unbounded tenderness did not prevent Hawthorne's shrewd sister-in-law from knowing that Delia "suffered . . . from the fear that I would steal her secret [the Shakespearean cipher] and publish it myself."

In her twenties and early thirties Delia's character partook apparently of the Victorian image of a perfect lady. She was a virtuous daughter and sister, religious, nice to the point of prudishness in her relations with the opposite sex. Had it not been for her almost excessive refinement she might have earned a reputation for strong-mindedness through her evident indifference to male admiration. Throughout her youth she gave no sign of having any interest in men at all, save those included in her immediate family. At fifteen she had decided to become a teacher, but she soon discovered that classroom instruction did not promise the kind of rewards that she wanted. She attempted a school of her own as Miss Beecher had done so successfully, but the venture failed and she wavered to writing. She had an errant fancy, could tell a tale with spirit, define a character and summon up a landscape with poetic immediacy. She tackled historical romance and did not scruple to write drama in verse. *Tales of the Puritans* and *The Bride of Fort Edward* were published and brought her neither fame nor fortune, but they led ultimately to the lecture platform. Delia had a remarkable propensity for oratory and was, like her brother, capable of haranguing an audience for hours together without tiring either it or herself.

The wives and daughters of her brother's colleagues were in transports about her. She lectured on classical antiquity, the Renaissance, and English letters in Boston, Hartford, and New Haven; her select audience of wellborn, well-endowed ladies paid highly for the privilege of hearing her. As she stood before two statues of Diana and Apollo (tributes from admiring listeners), fragile and fiery, dressed always in black which set off her delicate style of beauty to perfection, she struck the spectators as a Tennysonian princess, an enchanting priestess in the courts of the muses.

While Delia was in the way of accumulating, if not a fortune, a pretty good living and the literary fame that she had so passionately longed for as a schoolgirl, she was not the only woman in New Haven aspiring to literary eminence. At 77 Elm Street a young rival was putting the polish on a series of lustrous attainments. Henrietta Blake was at this time in her early twenties, a tall, dark girl of formidable achievement. She was a good classical scholar and is reliably reported to have thrown over an eligible *parti* for sending her a Greek ode disfigured by false quantities.

Unlike Delia Bacon she was born rich, one of the ten children of Eli Whitney Blake, inventor of the Blake stone crusher. Eli Whitney's cotton gin also loomed in her background. According to one of her admirers, James Hadley, she "avowed and gloried in a delightful perversity of taste."

The Blakes shared with the Bacons, the Taylors, the Days, the Baldwins, the Woolseys, and others a comfortable eminence in the New Haven hierarchy, and it was toward this company that the Reverend Alexander MacWhorter, the only son of a doting widow from New Jersey, directed his innocent footsteps. Possessing a good income, a good profile, and an engaging address, the gentle youth made a charming impression. Nathaniel Taylor took him under his special protection, and Leonard Bacon's signature was one of those adorning the articles licensing him to preach. He had won a reputation as scholar during his undergraduate days at Yale and was considered to have a pretty, if slightly condescending, wit. Beyond these attractions he seems to have had, in common with Delia Bacon, an indefinable allure. People flocked around him, especially men, although women liked him too. He claimed an extreme naïveté where women were concerned, but he took pains that no false quantities should mar his interchange with Henrietta Blake.

On becoming a licentiate in the Congregational Church, he moved into the same boardinghouse where Delia Bacon lived, fixed his large eyes on her, and breathed a longing to know her. The recipient of this confidence was a classmate, Robert W. Forbes, for whom Delia had conceived one of her celebrated dislikes. She considered him flimsy and quite unfit to

CONTINUED ON PAGE 88

churches—left to right: the Episcopal, the Center (or First), and a second Congregational church beyond.

15

FACES FROM THE PAST—V

"My lamp is nearly burned out," he admitted, "and the last glimmer has come." For the past two years not a day had passed when he was free of pain; one lung was gone, the other diseased; he was tormented alternately by dropsy and diarrhea, racked by chills and fever. He sat quietly in the armchair, saving himself, a wasted figure in an old-fashioned, snuff-colored coat with high stiff collar. Beside him were his Bible, a hymnal, and writing materials; too poor to hire a secretary, and almost blind, he nevertheless did what he could to answer the flood of correspondence he received. The hand of death was on him, and each day the procession of visitors increased—people who came to say farewell and to look into the old warrior's face for the last time. The king of France sent the popular artist Healy to paint his portrait before it was too late; photographers came to take daguerreotypes.

Little remained now but the iron will—that and the memories. Occasionally a remark by an old friend would set his mind to roaming back and forth across the years, and once again he would be Andy Jackson, nine years old and "public reader" in the Waxhaws of South Carolina. Clustered about him were thirty or more neighbors, listening gravely while the shrill voice proclaimed the news from Philadelphia: "In Congress, July 4, 1776. The Unanimous Declaration of the Thirteen United States of America. When, in the course of human events . . ."

Always there had been people around him. On the day that ended the "reign" of "King Andrew," after Mr. Van Buren had delivered his inaugural address, the ex-President descended the steps of the Capitol. And as he did a roar burst from the huge crowd, a roar of affection and gratitude and admiration such as few men have been privileged to hear. Halfway down the great steps General Jackson uncovered and bowed, and the cheers died away. Two days later the people of Washington turned out again, this time to bid him good-by. They lined the streets, overflowed the railroad depot, and spread out across the tracks, waiting silently at every vantage point that offered a glimpse of him. Andrew Jackson stood on the rear platform, his white mane blowing in the breeze, and the hushed crowd that watched the train chuffing out of sight felt, one man said, "as if a bright star had gone out of the sky."

Sometimes now, sitting alone in his bedroom, watching the dawn come, the dying man remembered how the fog had lifted from a field of cane stubble below New Orleans and how, through the patches, he had seen the scarlet-coated regulars heading across the frosty ground, crossbelts ghostly white in the morning light, thousands of bayonets weaving and bobbing as they moved relentlessly and unwittingly toward the point where he had massed his reserve. They were only five hundred yards distant when his cannon opened on them, three hundred yards away and running forward when his riflemen fired, and of five thousand men, just twenty reached his lines. When the American guns were silent, the General looked out across the cane field again and saw five hundred British getting to their feet from the heaps of dead comrades, the quick rising up all over the plain to come forward as prisoners. It looked, he recalled, like the day of resurrection, and it was his proudest hour. Forty years earlier he had learned to hate the British; before he was fourteen the War for Independence cost him his mother and two brothers, and an English officer's sword scarred him for life. Alone in the world, he made up his mind that everyone who was not for him was against him.

Daniel Webster once said, "He does what he thinks is right, and does it with all his might," and the old man would not argue with that. There had been some good men up against him—Clay, Calhoun, Nicholas Biddle, Webster himself—and he had beaten them all. When he left the White House he had but two regrets, he told a friend: He had not been able to shoot Henry Clay or hang John C. Calhoun. It was not enough for a man to be right; he had to be tough—you learned that fighting Indians and Englishmen. He remembered how he got the nickname: he and his Tennesseeans were on the march, hacking a road through swamps, building bridges as they went, and a lot of his boys were sick and hungry. While he walked up and down the length of the long column, encouraging them, seeing that they had rations, looking after them, one soldier had stared after him and said admiringly, "He's tough." "Tough as hickory," added another, and the name had stuck.

And Old Hickory became the spokesman for the frontier—partly because the frontier badly needed one just then, but also because the frontier wanted toughness and honesty and directness in its leaders and because Andrew Jackson feared no man. Once when he and the Bentons were feuding, Tom and Jesse Benton arrived in Nashville wearing pistols; Jackson walked into town with a riding whip and went looking for them. Once again he challenged Charles Dickinson, one of the best shots in Tennessee, to a duel, and even after Dickinson put a bullet next to his heart he stood there, slowly took aim, and shot his opponent down. "I should have hit him," he said, "if he had shot me through the brain." Thirty-nine years later Dickinson's bullet was still in his chest; the pistol that killed Dickinson still lay on the mantel of Jackson's bedroom. In his will he left a sword to his nephew, asking, characteristically, "that he fail not to use it when necessary in support and protection of our glorious Union."

Long after he died, someone asked Alfred, one of his slaves, if he thought his master would get into Heaven on Judgment Day. Alfred knew his man. "If Gen'l Jackson takes it into his head to git to Heaven," he said, "who's gwine to keep him out?"
—*Richard M. Ketchum*

The Old Showman's Last Triumph

Near the close of a gaudy career, P.T. Barnum took the "greatest show on earth" to London. His scrapbook reveals the master of hokum at the top of his form

No one ever accused Phineas Taylor Barnum of being modest. For more than fifty years this self-acknowledged "prince of humbugs" so thoroughly fooled, fleeced, and entertained the American public that the name Barnum itself became as famous as the artists and oddities he put on display. Jenny Lind, General Tom Thumb, the Bearded Lady, the Siamese Twins, Jo-Jo the Dog-Faced Boy, Jumbo the Elephant, human and animal rarities of every description—from them he had fashioned an endlessly diverting drama, with himself never far from the center of the stage.

By 1889 Barnum could offer his own life as proof that virtue survives adversity. After middle age a nondrinker and nonsmoker, he preached abstinence and never failed to emphasize the wholesomeness and moral uplift of his shows, even as he genially confessed to his mercenary intentions. "Every crowd has a silver lining," said Barnum. Twice his prodigious American Museum in New York burned to the ground, but Barnum always bounced back—secure in his self-esteem, his grip on the popular imagination—and at his death in 1891 he was worth four million dollars.

But two years before had come the capstone of his career. Urged on by his partner, James Anthony Bailey, despite his own doubts that it would pay, Barnum took a combined circus and pageant to London for a hundred-day engagement at the Olympia Amphitheater. His fears that English audiences might not welcome him were groundless; he was a stupendous success. Fifteen thousand people attended the opening; the newspapers praised him extravagantly; royalty came; a banquet for two hundred prominent persons was held in his honor; the talk of London was nothing but Barnum, Barnum, Barnum.

On his return, the aging impresario made a scrapbook for his favorite daughter, Caroline, filled with programs, press clippings, cartoons, and other mementos of the glorious event. From this album, now in the collection of Jack Winsten of Bridgeport, Connecticut, AMERICAN HERITAGE has assembled the portfolio on the pages that follow, an echo from the circus world of clowns and curiosities, of tents and tanbark, to which Barnum's name is still indissolubly bound.
—*Eric Larrabee*

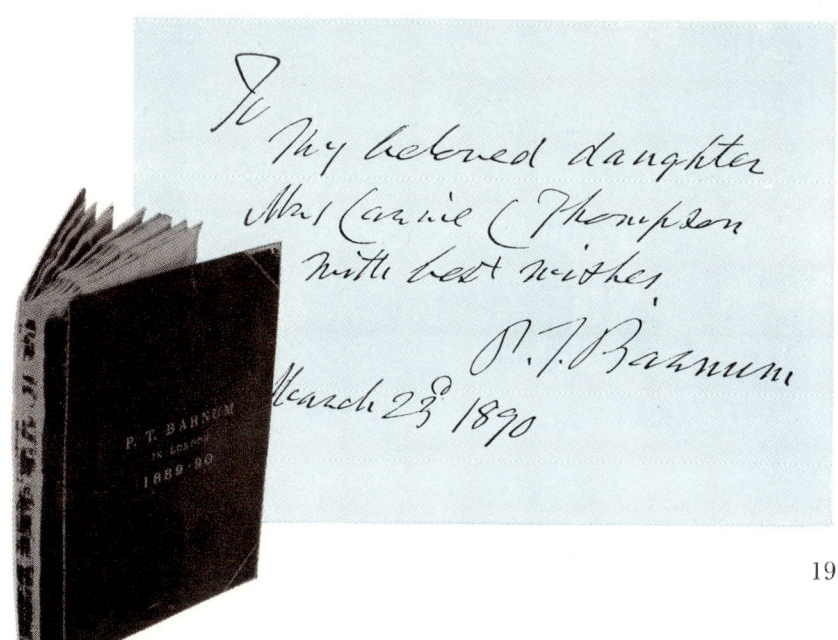

Inside the cover of Barnum's London program (left) he promised to avoid "bombast or exaggeration," but words like "monster" and "colossal" somehow kept creeping in. His album for his daughter (right) is inscribed to her.

19

Barnum was always proud that his shows appealed to children, and went out of his way to emphasize that fact. "In America I am on famously friendly terms with all the Little Folks . . ." he wrote in a specially prepared album of the show; "I would rather be called the children's friend than the world's king." His album contains many of these gaily colored booklets for his young customers, like the Jumbo alphabet (above) with its *A* for Barnum's own Arrival in England (below). The scene itself must have been somewhat less sumptuous, but certainly no less exotic, when the steamship *Furnessia* disgorged on the London docks its load of performers, elephants, camels, zebras, horses, band wagons, Roman chariots, and innumerable trunks and chests—"as strange a cargo," noted *Harper's Weekly,* "as ever was loaded on a ship." To transport the circus across the ocean was costing Barnum and Bailey $350,000, and they had contracted to pay the Olympia $12,000 a day for a hundred days. It was thus a somewhat apprehensive Barnum who had finally set sail aboard the *Etruria* with his British-born wife, Nancy.

One reason for Barnum's uneasiness was his fear that the British public would still resent his purchase of the elephant Jumbo, seven years before, from the London Zoological Gardens. Jumbo was one of the largest pachyderms in captivity; his daily intake of food included two hundred pounds of hay, fifteen loaves of bread, five pails of water, and a quart of whiskey. He was the Gardens' major attraction, and when the news of his sale became public, there had been a storm of indignation.

Patriotic Britons (and their children) flooded the newspapers with letters protesting Jumbo's departure. It was as though someone had tried to sell a national monument. Jumbo became the major issue of the day. There were Jumbo hats, Jumbo cigars, Jumbo neckties. A magazine suggested that the motto on the British coat of arms be changed to "Dieu et mon Jumbo." The American envoy, James Russell Lowell, said in a speech that "the only burning question between England and America is Jumbo."

When the time came for Jumbo to leave, he himself intensified the orgy of public sentiment by lying down in the street and refusing to move. When Barnum's agent cabled, asking "What shall we do?" Barnum replied: "Let him lie there a week if he wants to. It is the best advertisement in the world." Eventually Jumbo—enclosed in a cage, placated with beer, and lifted aboard ship by steam crane—made his way to the United States, where he justified Barnum's sagacity by earning $1,750,000 in his first season.

But tragedy followed. On the night of September 15, 1885, in St. Thomas, Ontario, Jumbo was struck by a freight train. Though the locomotive and two cars were demolished, poor Jumbo, alas, did not survive. The world was saddened, but Barnum was not exactly inconsolable. He proceeded to have Jumbo's skeleton mounted and his hide stuffed, with the result (right) that he could now exhibit two Jumbos at once.

GRAND JUMBO
NOW RETURNS TO YOU
A DOUBLE PRODIGY, AND SCIENCE'S MOST MAJESTIC TRIUMPH.

The tragic death of Jumbo the Great, who was killed by a freight train, at St. Thomas, Canada, Sept. 15th, 1885, in the heroic and successful effort to save Matthew Scott, his beloved companion and keeper, and his dear little comrade, the dwarf Clown Elephant, "Tom Thumb," was regarded as almost a public calamity, and evoked world-wide sorrow. That

THE BIGGEST AND BEST-LOVED BEAST KNOWN TO MAN

IS NOT A MEMORY
BUT STILL A STUPENDOUS REALITY

is due to the patient efforts and rare scientific skill of the distinguished Naturalist and Scientist, Prof. HENRY A. WARD, of Rochester, N. Y., who, after months of arduous labor, triumphantly succeeded in perpetuating Jumbo in unimpaired grandeur of presence and absolute perfection of form, so that we not only exhibit

THE COLOSSAL LORD OF ALL THE BEASTS
AS NATURAL AND IMPOSING AS IN LIFE

But in strange and most WONDERFUL ADDITION, and standing at his side,

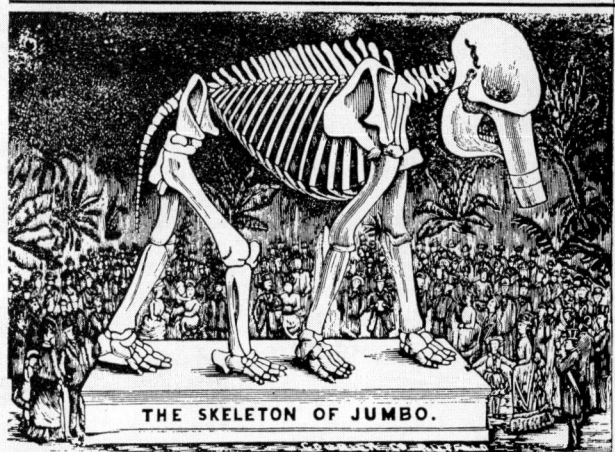

THE SKELETON OF JUMBO.

JUMBO'S PERFECT AND TREMENDOUS SKELETON

Complete in all its Vast and Massive Parts, and THE WORLD'S MOST GIGANTIC AND AMAZING PHYSICAL NOVELTY.

TWO MARVELOUSLY STUPENDOUS AND NOVEL FEATURES

Which have excited the wonder and admiration of Millions in America, as they will assuredly do here.

WE HAVE BEEN REPEATEDLY
OFFERED A BIG FORTUNE FOR THEM

HUGE HISTORICAL TABLEAUX

HEATHEN RELIGIOUS RITES

Tremendous Scenes of Conflict

BARBARIC RICHES OF THE ORIENT

ECLIPSING ANY HUNDRED THEATRES

FLOODS OF SONG AND MUSIC

Pageants of Prismatic Hues

HOLIDAY ASSEMBLAGES AND FETES

Sports of the Circus Maximus

The POMP OF ROME'S VICTORIOUS LEGIONS

Grand Procession

Stupendous Historical Dramatic Spectacle, **NERO;** OR THE **DESTRUCTION OF ROME**
Testing the full capacity of the Largest Steamships to transport it.

Long before Hollywood discovered *Ben Hur,* Barnum (and his collaborator the Hungarian impresario Imre Kiralfy) had realized the advantage of a pageant based upon imperial Rome—namely, that it combines the theme of Christian heroism with scenes of lip-smacking decadence. "Nero; or the Destruction of Rome" was no exception. "A grand show," the London *Mirror* called it. "It surpasses anything of the kind ever attempted in this or any other country." There was something in it for everybody, from a triumphal procession (above) and bacchanalian orgies through to gladiatorial contests and chariot races (right). To judge by his press notices, Barnum's audiences had never before been exposed to anything at once so educational and so stupefying. "It is no mere artificial show," rhapsodized the London *Chronicle,* "but a vivid and vast realization of life."

Nero through Rome.

GIANT STAGE OF BLAZING PANTOMIME

NERO'S OLYMPIAN TRIUMPH

DAZZLING VIEWS OF IMPERIAL ORGIES

Festivals of the "Eternal City"

REFLEX OF THE REGAL ROME THAT WAS

Her Towering Temples, Palaces and Walls

Grand Gladiatorial Combats

MOST STUPENDOUS, GLORIOUS DISPLAYS

COLOSSAL, DAZZLING BALLETS

SPLENDID MIRROR OF THE CLASSIC AGE

Early in his career Barnum learned a lesson he never forgot: get the upper classes on your side and the masses will follow. When he had brought Tom Thumb to London in 1844, he had secured an audience for the midget with Queen Victoria; after that he had only to sit back and collect the receipts. Now in 1889 royalty came to his circus. The Prince of Wales came (the Princess came four times), bringing his young son who would one day be George V. (When Barnum asked the boy if he was going to stay until the end of the performance, he looked around cautiously and said, "Mr. Barnum, I shall remain here until they sing God Save Grandmother.") Barnum seems to have appealed to aristocrats partly because he was a curiosity, but partly also because in his simple way he could be familiar without being insolent. For him the high point must have been the banquet in his honor with a guest list (below) filled with names from *Burke's Peerage* and *Who's Who*, among them Lord Randolph Churchill, Sir Robert Peel, Henry Irving, and Oscar Wilde. His health was proposed by the editor of the *Pall Mall Gazette*, who compared Barnum favorably with Napoleon Bonaparte, Julius Caesar, and Alexander the Great, since they were showmen too, but made their shows out of human misery instead, as Barnum did, out of innocent pleasure. Also included in the toasts was another group whose good will P. T. Barnum never allowed to go unremembered: the ever-helpful Press.

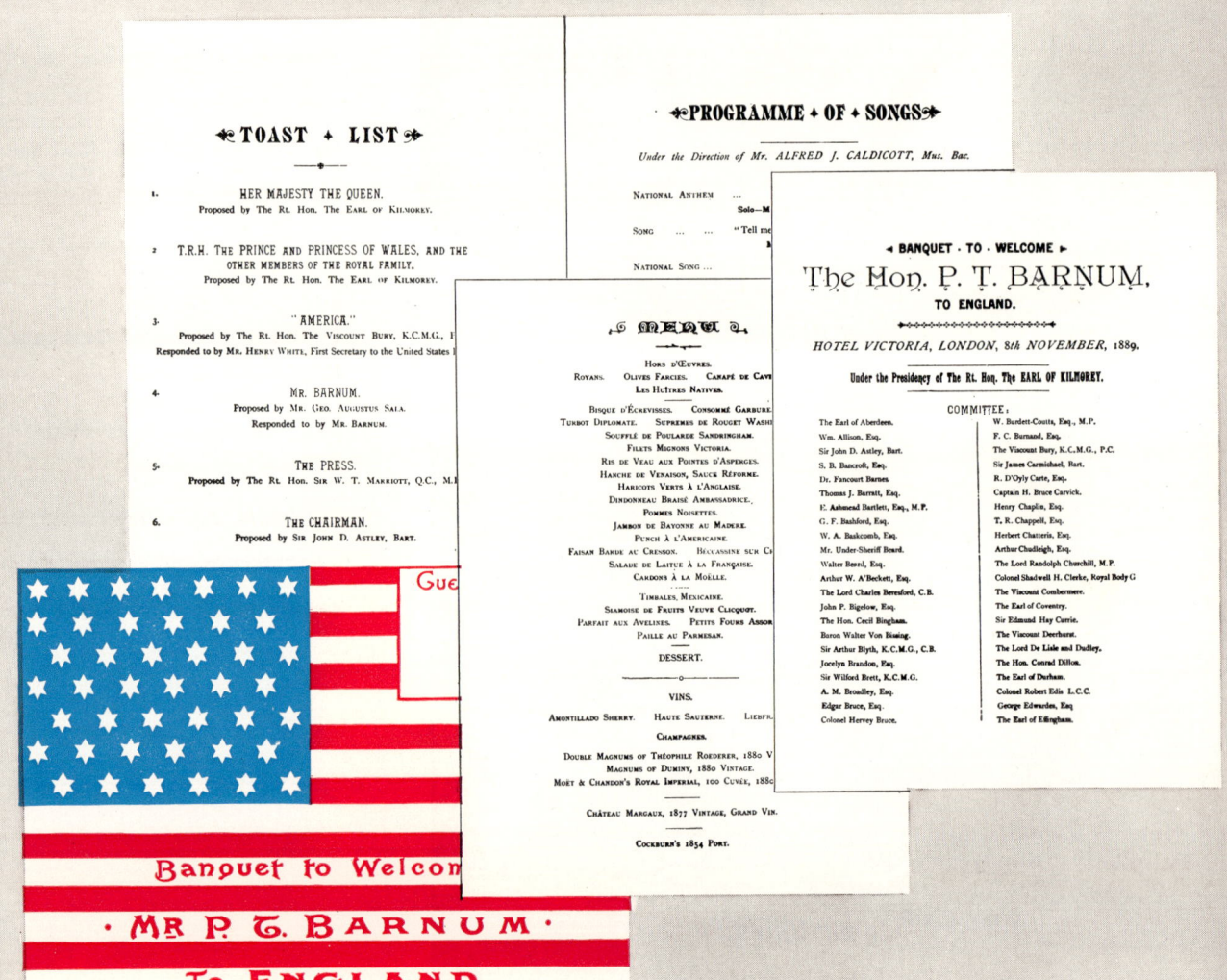

On his return home, Barnum shrewdly capitalized on the social lions he had tamed abroad.

SOME PERFORMANCES IN THE CIRCUS

There is a popular misconception that Barnum invented the circus. Actually he was first of all a museum man. He may have given the modern circus much of its character, but he did not become a full-time circus proprietor until he was sixty. When he encountered a vigorous young competitor named James A. Bailey, he decided to join what he couldn't lick; result: Barnum & Bailey.

Performing Stallions and Ponies.

But amidst the acrobats, the ringmaster, and the trained horses, Barnum still remained a major attraction. Most days at the Olympia, the performance stopped while the old man circled the arena in his open carriage. At intervals he would halt, rise, remove his shiny top hat, and say in his squeaky voice, "I suppose you all come to see Barnum. Wa-al, I'm Barnum."

THE CELEBRATED TROUPE

The elephants and the clown—the grotesque of nature and the foolishness of man—fittingly symbolize Barnum's stock in trade. Given a good show, he knew

PERFORMING ELEPHANTS.

that the crowds would always come flocking to his call. Humbug he may indeed have been, but without malice, and he helped America learn to laugh at itself.

THE WATER WAR

By REMI NADEAU

"There was a mighty hissing roar and down the great spillway dashed the foaming liquid." So an eyewitness described the scene above, on November 5, 1913, as William Mulholland triumphantly opened his aqueduct.

As Owens Valley water came down the aqueduct, thirsty Los Angeles rejoiced. But angry farmers were buying dynamite and cleaning guns

TITLE INSURANCE AND TRUST COMPANY, LOS ANGELES

Beyond the Missouri River, water has been almost a sacred commodity—accorded the same passionate respect that it received in the Bible lands. There is an old saying in the West: "Steal my horse, carry off my wife, but don't touch my water." Ever since the American frontier reached the great bend of the Missouri, water—or the lack of it—has been the chief determinant of western development. And from the time that the first farmer fenced a water hole on the open range, it has been the West's chief source of conflict. Texas and New Mexico contended over the Rio Grande. Colorado battled Kansas over the Arkansas River, then turned to fight Wyoming for the North Platte. California took on all comers in the struggle for the Colorado River.

Ordinarily, these epic contests were fought in the realm of water law. Throughout most of the Far West, this body of law was based on the miner's code of "first in use, first in right"—even though the benefited land was not contiguous to the water source. But in California, water law flowed from two origins—the priority rights established by the early American miners, and the riparian rights for contiguous land, according to the Spanish tradition and the English common law.

The complications brought on by this clash of two traditions intensified the water struggle in California and put a premium on legal cunning. While most western fights over water took place in the courtroom or the legislative hall, Californians fought many of theirs outside the law because one side or another distrusted legal machinery. This was the basis of violence in the Los Angeles-Owens Valley conflict. Not only was it the most savage water war in United States history; it provided an early warning of a disturbing modern trend—the inability of outlying communities to protect their identity and their way of life from being swallowed by Megalopolis.

In the long drought that afflicted California from 1892 to 1904, the burgeoning city of Los Angeles appeared to have reached its limit at a population of approximately 200,000. City parks and residential lawns were allowed to dry up. Irrigation canals were commandeered to supply drinking water. If Los Angeles could not find a new water source—and quickly—it would no longer be able to absorb the steady tide of newcomers from the Midwest. To the Los Angeles boosters, such a catastrophe was unthinkable.

One man stepped forward to lead the Angelenos out of their dilemma. William Mulholland, an Irish immigrant, had arrived in 1877 with ten dollars in his pocket and the resolve to "grow with the country." Within nine years he had become superintendent of the company supplying water to the city, and when the company was purchased by Los Angeles in 1902, Mulholland was placed in charge of the entire waterworks. He had risen by hard work, by diligent study of engineering books late into the night, and—most important—by sheer force of personality. His supreme self-confidence inspired city authorities to act upon his recommendations alone, without further study. "They have always been," he once said, "in the habit of taking my word."

With this kind of authority, Mulholland charged forth in

This photograph of one of the monster siphons that took the water over the Sierras indicates the scope of the construction job. Engineers had to build a tramway to deliver the huge pipe sections—up to ten feet across and some of them more than an inch thick. Concrete for the piers (cement came from a specially erected plant) was mixed on the site.

LOS ANGELES DEPT. OF WATER AND POWER

the late summer of 1904 to combat the city's water shortage. Since local sources were already tapped, he looked afield for a new supply. His friend Fred Eaton, a former Los Angeles mayor, had once told him of a magnificent water source on the east side of the Sierra Nevadas. Desperately, he now asked Eaton to show it to him.

In September the two friends climbed into a two-horse buckboard and headed north. Camping in the open, they drove 250 miles over a rutted wagon road across the Mojave Desert to Owens Valley. Through this green oasis, nestled against the east scarp of the High Sierra like some remote Alpine vale, flowed stream upon stream of fresh snow water. They converged into the Owens River, which coursed down the valley and lost itself in the alkaline pollution of Owens Lake, one of the world's rare dead seas.

In the 1860's pioneer American farmers had wrested the valley from the Paiute Indians, and by the seventies were beginning to divert water from the river and its tributaries into large canals to irrigate the land. By the time Mulholland reached the valley in 1904, he found a population of some five thousand and a small empire—about 38,000 acres—of fruit orchards, melon vines, and cool alfalfa. It was truly a "land flowing with milk and honey."

But in the meandering river and its feeder streams Mulholland saw only one thing: enough water to supply two million people and allow his own stunted city to grow into a giant. What was more, according to Fred Eaton's rough calculations, the river could be diverted around Owens Lake and brought south all the way to Los Angeles by gravity, without the aid of a single pump.

It would, of course, be years before the city would grow enough to use the entire flow of the river. But in the meantime, to maintain title to the water under the law of prior use, the surplus could be used by farmers in San Fernando Valley, adjacent to Los Angeles. The whole project would represent the biggest municipal aqueduct in the world—a breathtaking project for a self-educated engineer. Immediately, Mulholland was captured by the boldness of Fred Eaton's concept. "When I saw it staring me in the face," he later declared, "I couldn't back away from it." While Mulholland sold the plan to Los Angeles authorities, Eaton went through lower Owens Valley lining up riparian water rights.

Trouble loomed in the valley's own ambitions for water development. The young United States Reclamation Service, founded by Theodore Roosevelt in 1902, had proposed a dam in the Owens River gorge to store water for irrigating the valley below. Its isolation and its limited area would keep the region from becoming a major agricultural empire like the one being carved out in the Imperial Valley. But by providing an assured water supply year in and year out, the proposed reclamation project would certainly bring to Owens Valley a new order of life and prosperity. In this clash of interests the city had a key ally. The chief Reclamation Service engineer for the Southwest was J. B. Lippincott, a friend of Eaton and Mulholland, and by "religion" an ardent Los Angeles booster. At his insistence, consideration of the Owens River reclamation project was abandoned to make way for the city's water plans.

When the Los Angeles *Times* broke the news in July, 1905, of a "Titanic Project to Give City a River," there were two distinct reactions. Among the boosters there was immediate jubilation: the city's wonderful growth would not be halted for lack of water! Within hours, property in much of the county doubled in price.

But in Owens Valley a different reaction greeted the *Times* story. All at once its people saw their reclamation dream go glimmering. Fred Eaton and his son, finishing some last-minute affairs in the valley town of Bishop, saw an ugly mob gathering around them in the street. They hurriedly packed and drove their buggy out of town, but before he escaped, Eaton was told that he would "never take the water out of the valley" and that if he came back he would be drowned in the river.

Nor was valley anger cooled by reports that water which Los Angeles did not actually need for the next few years would be used for irrigating the San Fernando Valley. As early as 1903, a syndicate of Los Angeles entrepreneurs had taken an option on a large chunk of that valley. Not very long afterward it was joined by Moses H. Sherman, who was a member of the Board of Water Commissioners. After Mulholland outlined his aqueduct plan to city officials, but before it was publicly announced, the syndicate exercised its option and bought 16,200 acres. The land thus purchased at approximately $30 an acre was to soar to $300 an acre. Today it is valued by the front foot. When operations of the syndicate were made public in 1905, Owens Valley people believed they were the victims of an outrageous water grab for the benefit of a few land schemers. Awaiting their chance, they moved to block Mulholland when he asked for a right of way for his proposed aqueduct across federal lands. "Not one drop for irrigation!" they shouted, pointing to the San Fernando deal.

The battle that followed raged from the floor of Congress to the White House. To prevent profiteering on the water itself, President Roosevelt proposed an amendment to the right-of-way bill that would prohibit Los Angeles from selling water to corporations or individuals for resale. Thus altered, the right-of-way bill passed Congress in June, 1906. But it contained no prohibition against the use of Owens River water for irrigation in the San Fernando Valley.

Inspired by this victory, the Angelenos moved to consolidate their water gains in Owens Valley. Once again the federal government was called upon for help. To forestall private claimants who might harass the city's program, the Reclamation Service had continued to bar entry to public lands that had been within its abandoned project. But this did not include most of the flatland of the valley. The Angelenos thereupon asked Chief Forester Gifford Pinchot to extend national-forest boundaries to include the valley, even though the Forest Service Law forbade the reservation of land more valuable "for agricultural purposes than for forest purposes."

Owens Valley people were outraged. Throughout the region, they cried, the only trees were those they themselves had planted. Nevertheless, in April of 1908 Pinchot's decree extending the Sierra Forest Reserve was signed by the President. The city was tightening its grip. "Los Angeles has been given all that she asked for," groaned one valley editor, adding ominously, "except the water."

But the intrepid Mulholland, who had secured $25,000,000 in two bond elections to finance the big ditch, was already in the field turning the earth.

Over most of the 240-mile route he faced a forbidding desert, devoid of the necessities of life, innocent of supply lines, crisscrossed by jagged mountains, and cursed with brutal heat. Fortunately the rugged Irishman thrived on challenge. Since steam power

William Mulholland—"the Chief"—built his ditch in five years, as he promised, and under the $25,000,000 budget.

At the height of the water war, on May 27, 1927, Owens Valley farmers blew up a 450-foot section of No Name siphon. The repair bill came to $500,000. When dynamiters struck again at another spot the following night, the city sent in armed guards. But the destruction continued.

was impractical over this arid route, he built two hydroelectric plants in Owens Valley and strung 169 miles of transmission lines—making his aqueduct the first major engineering project in the United States constructed principally by electric power. He solved part of the hauling problem by building another plant near the line of march to supply the million barrels of cement he estimated he would need. And for the heavy transportation the Southern Pacific Railroad took a hand and built a standard-gauge branch line northward into Owens Valley.

Then, over sterile wasteland and through mountain ranges, Mulholland drove his giant ditch. Along the whole line the monumental work was accomplished with new engineering triumphs. Digging his tunnels, particularly the five-mile Elizabeth Tunnel that bored through the Coast Range into southern California, Mulholland's crew equaled, then repeatedly raised, the world's hardrock drilling record. To take water across the deep canyons of the Sierra foothills the ditch was converted into monstrous inverted siphons—one of them built to withstand a greater head of water than any other pipe in the nation. Hauling sections of steel pipe to this siphon from the nearest rail point required wagon teams of fifty-two mules each.

By the middle of 1912, in spite of physical obstacles, financial problems, and labor discontent, Mulholland was able to report to the city that "the end of our task seems fairly in sight." But he was nearly exhausted from tension and overwork. "If it were not for looking ahead to the time of reward . . ." he once said, "I could not go on with the work, for I am worn out."

That time came on November 5, 1913, when Mulholland's big ditch was put into operation with a huge ceremony at the northwest corner of San Fernando Valley. At the point where the aqueduct came through the mountains, an artificial cascade had been built to display the water as it splashed into the valley. To this spot on the appointed day came thousands of Angelenos—by carriage, auto, and train. Around a flag-draped platform they gathered for the preliminary speeches; above on the mountainside a crew of men stood at the gates, ready to crank wheels that would release the first Owens River water. Mulholland himself gave them the signal by unfurling the Stars and Stripes on a flagpole. The assembly cheered, cannons boomed, a brass band played furiously. Down the causeway came a torrent of water—foaming, dancing, churning, spraying its mist over the nearest bystanders. Without waiting for the presentation speeches the entire multitude rushed to the side of the cascade. Left virtually without an audience, the exuberant Mulholland turned to the mayor, who was to receive the water on behalf of the city, and made the five-word speech that has become famous:

"There it is. Take it."

In this triumphant moment Los Angeles—and all of California—turned to shower adulation on William Mulholland. The aqueduct was recognized across the country as the finest in the United States. As an engineering feat it was second only to the great Panama Canal. The University of California gave Mulholland an honorary doctor's degree, and he was introduced everywhere as "the Goethals of the West" and as "California's greatest man."

Virtually overnight, Los Angeles moved from water famine to water flood. The San Fernando Valley was transformed from a grain-raising community dependent on intermittent rainfall to an empire of truck gardens and orchards—one of the richest agricultural communities in the nation. In 1915 practically the entire valley joined the city. With their sure water supply as a lure, the Los Angeles boosters were able to annex one community after another to create the biggest municipal area in the world.

But for all his engineering genius, Mulholland had omitted one vital feature from his Owens River project—a major reservoir. In his anxiety to get water to the city, he had simply diverted the river to Los Angeles; the only reservoirs were those necessary for the month-to-month operation of the aqueduct. He had, it was true, tapped the river below the valley's main center of agriculture, so that under ordinary circumstances both farmers and city dwellers would have enough water. But without a reservoir there was no means of storing the precipitation of the wet years; when the dry years came, there was insufficient water to supply both the city and the valley. Upon this predicament the Owens Valley water war was reborn, and it was to become more savage than ever.

The obvious site for such a reservoir was the same that had been planned for the ill-fated federal reclamation project. A dam located in the Owens River gorge upstream from the valley, above the town of Bishop, would back up a magnificent lake in Long Valley. Fred Eaton, who owned the site, had offered to sell it to Los Angeles for something like a million dollars. But Mulholland, believing his friend was trying to take advantage of the city, refused. Eaton then gave up an easement for a reservoir that could have been created by a hundred-foot dam, but such a reservoir was too small to serve as a year-to-year regulator. When the city began constructing the dam anyway, the settlers of Owens Valley filed an injunction suit: they would never stand for a dam on their river unless it was big enough to assure water for all. Caught between Fred Eaton and the valley farmers, Los Angeles abandoned its dam. The Owens River was left uncontrolled, and the first dry spell set the city and the valley at each other's throats.

By 1923 the great aqueduct that had been built for fifty years of growth was already proving inadequate. Los Angeles, enjoying its biggest real-estate boom, had outgrown its old rival, San Francisco. In the lush San Fernando Valley the farmers would have used almost the entire flow of the aqueduct in the summer months if Mulholland had not arbitrarily shut off irrigation water.

Desperate for water, Mulholland invaded Owens

CONTINUED ON PAGE 103

The leaders of the opposition were Mark (left) and Wilfred W. Watterson, whose banks held mortgages on many of the valley's farms. When they were jailed for speculating with bank funds in the fall of 1927, the farmers were left leaderless.

"I have built me a little cottage on the banks of the Hudson," Irving wrote to Charles Dickens in 1841. Before he died in 1859 he enlarged Sunnyside into the "elegant little snuggery" seen in this Currier & Ives lithograph. There, seated on the porch (below) or strolling in the gardens, he supervised "a happy household of young nieces" and entertained the rich and the famous. Subsequently restored, by a Rockefeller grant, the house is now open to the public.

THE SUNNY MASTER OF SUNNYSIDE

By CURTIS DAHL

Blending satire and nostalgia, Washington Irving taught his readers both to love the past and chuckle over its absurdities

"I seek only to blow a flute accompaniment in the national concert, and leave others to play the fiddle and the French horn." So wrote Washington Irving early in his long career:

I have attempted no lofty theme, nor sought to look wise and learned, which appears to be very much the fashion among our American writers, at present. I have preferred addressing myself to the feelings and fancy of the reader more than to his judgment. My writings, therefore, may appear light and trifling in our country of philosophers and politicians. But if they possess merit in the class of literature to which they belong, it is all to which I aspire in the work.

Today Irving's candid appraisal of his own work seems a valid one. He was never to be profound. He was always to appeal to the "feelings and fancy" of his readers more than to their intellects. Yet the charm of his personality and the geniality of his style enabled him to blow such a graceful and popular "flute accompaniment" to the deeper diapasons of his era that he became one of the most influential figures in the history of American literature.

Perhaps no American author, with the possible exception of Longfellow, was so genuinely beloved as Irving in his time. On the day of his funeral in 1859, New York City courts adjourned, flags were hung at half-mast, and all the bells of the city tolled their grief. Thousands of people in England as well as America felt that they had lost a friend. But few mourned Irving's passing more than his fellow writers in America. They remembered how, at great personal sacrifice, he had given up his notes on the conquest of Mexico to Prescott; how he had arranged for the first publication of William Cullen Bryant's poems in England; and too, how he had been America's most effective literary ambassador to Europe. As one contemporary commented, "The older authors felt that a friend, not a rival—the younger, that a father—had gone."

From the beginning of his career as a writer, Irving had won a tremendous popularity in America. His first major work, *A History of New York by Diedrich Knickerbocker,* published in 1809 when he was twenty-six, had scored an instant success. Despite the objections of some descendants of old Dutch families to the frivolous way in which Irving had treated their ancestors, Diedrich (according to one observer) "excited an interest in the metropolis never before roused up by any literary occurrence; scarcely, perhaps, by any public event." Irving himself, modest though he always was, admitted that the book "took" the town. Soon he had become a literary lion in New York and was being read not only in the drawing rooms of the city but even in the log huts of the frontier. His next important work, *The Sketch Book of Geoffrey Crayon*, which appeared ten years later, was just as successful. Though the later books never enjoyed quite the vogue of these two, Irving never lost the admiration of his vast American public. Returning home in 1832 after seventeen years in Europe, he was greeted as a national hero. All the outstanding literary men of New York attended the public dinner given to honor him. The papers were full of his praises. At various times he was offered the nomination for mayor of New York, the nomination for candidate for Congress, and the opportunity to become Secretary of the Navy under Martin Van Buren. He declined all. But when Secretary of State Webster appointed him minister to Spain in 1842, he accepted, and all America rejoiced in its new envoy.

The first American writer to win wide acclaim in Europe, Irving was as popular abroad as at home. In England, with the publication of his early successes, he was accepted in the most refined intellectual circles. He became the fast friend of the poet Tom Moore. Samuel Rogers, whose literary breakfasts were far more memorable than his poetry, invited him to his table. He wandered across the romantic Scottish moors with Sir Walter Scott. He met William Wordsworth. Byron was heard to say that Irving's writings were his delight and that he knew *Geoffrey Crayon* by heart. Royalty in England, Spain, France, and Germany also received Irving. When he was given a Doctor of Laws degree at Oxford in June, 1830, the ceremony was almost drowned out by the roaring cheers from the undergraduates chanting the titles of his books. He was so well-known (or American history so little-known) that when a little English girl looked at a statue of George Washington and asked who he was, her mother answered, "Why, my dear, don't you know? He wrote the *Sketch Book!*"

The adulation that was showered on Irving at home was due in large part to the fact that his works so exactly fitted the needs and tastes of the time. America was no longer, as it had been in colonial days, a cluster of coastal settlements facing the perils of an illimitable wilderness. Nor was it any longer racked by a grim struggle for independence. By the 1820's, the internal discord that had disturbed the early days of the Republic was subsiding into what was to be known as the Era of Good Feelings. After years of hardship and war, after the struggle to set up a new form of government, Americans wished to relax. In literature as in so many other things, they were willing to accept gladly what an earlier generation might well have considered light and trifling.

There is perhaps no better illustration of this new attitude than the difference between Irving and his own father. If Irving was not the wise and learned author who had occupied the center of the stage during so much of earlier American history, it was no fault of Deacon William Irving. And if the elder Irving hoped for sober, God-fearing, and practical offspring, his son Washington (born in 1783, he was the youngest of a family of eleven) disappointed him. He paid little attention to school. Though he read his father's copies of Milton and *Pilgrim's Progress,* he preferred lighter literature, like *Don Quixote*. Even worse, he scrambled out of his bedroom window at night to attend the theater. He refused to be a minister and indeed, throughout his whole life, he never took formal religion seriously. When he studied law under Judge Hoffman, he wrote more essays than briefs and was far more interested in the pretty young Hoffman daughters (with one of whom, Matilda, he later fell in love) than in attorneys or clients.

Having passed his bar examinations (evidently through pull—one of the examiners admitted that he knew "damned little"), he did not practice but was installed in a comfortable nook at his brothers' importing firm, where his duties rarely interfered with his social and literary pursuits. Soon he became one of the leading members of a group of witty and talented young New Yorkers that came to be known as the Knickerbocker school. Like Irving, these young men had been born too late to remember the hardships of the Revolutionary War, when British soldiers had been billeted in many houses in the city and food had at times been hard to obtain. They represented a gayer generation that had rescued New York from the rusticity of its Dutch origin; it now rivaled Philadelphia in the sophistication of its culture.

Having broken away from their mother country, Americans at the beginning of the nineteenth century were eager to develop traditions and legends of their own. They wanted to find a past, an American past. Amateur archaeologists, among them Thomas Jefferson and Governor DeWitt Clinton of New York, attempted to unravel the mysteries of the ancient civilization of the Mound Builders. Other scholars studied the culture of the Indians, speculating as to their possible origin in the lost tribes of Israel and theorizing that perhaps the pyramids of the Aztecs had been influenced by the ancient Egyptians. Historians were assembling materials on the Revolutionary War, and Parson Weems—originator of the cherry tree story—had by 1800 already begun to build up the heroic myth of George Washington. Poets, too, were writing on the history and legends of the young republic.

Irving not only realized the desires of Americans of his time for legends of their own but also pioneered the very themes that were later to make American romantic writing great. His *History of New York* established a pattern that would be followed by Longfellow in his legends of Paul Revere and Miles Standish, and Hawthorne in his gloomy allegories of Puritan New England. In his *Life and Voyages of Christopher Columbus* and in his *Voyages and Discoveries of the Companions of Columbus,* Irving took up the themes of exploration and seafaring that Cooper and Melville were later to treat in more detail. Irving was one of the first to recognize that the Indian was also a fitting subject for American literature. His pictures of Indians in *The Sketch Book* precede both Cooper's Leatherstocking Tales and Longfellow's glorification of the noble savage in *Hiawatha*. Even more important, Irving was one of the first (in a literary sense) to "open up the West," with books like *Astoria*—a description of John Jacob Astor's fur empire in the Northwest—and *The Adventures of Captain Bonneville, U.S.A.* Furthermore, Irving saw a fertile field in the biography of national heroes; his five-volume *Life of George Washington* became a landmark in the developing legend of the father of his country.

But Irving did not limit himself to American themes. Much of his appeal lay in his love of high adventure and heroism in the long ago and far away. An age that idolized Lord Byron and Sir Walter Scott responded enthusiastically to Irving's dramatic pictures of the conquest of Granada, or the life and campaigns of Mahomet. For all the romance of foreign lands, however, his American stories remained his most popular works. His life of Columbus, which followed the rise and fall of the Admiral of the Ocean Sea, was welcomed as a part of the epic of America—as was his piece in the *Sketch Book* on King Philip—"Philip of Pokanoket"—which glorified a truly noble Indian leader.

But it is in his *Astoria*—a book written in large part out of patriotic pride—that Irving told his most exciting story of heroic American adventure. After his return from Europe in 1832, Irving had wanted to demonstrate that, despite his literary delight in the antiquities of England and Spain and Germany, his first loyalty was to America. Thus when John Jacob Astor offered him access to the records of the great fur-trading house which he headed, Irving jumped at the chance. The book that resulted is an exciting account of the treacherous and bloody competition of American and British fur companies, of the pageantry of life and death among the wild savages of the plains, and the incredible hardships of the mountain men who braved starvation, Indians, and wild animals among the defiles of the Rockies. Especially graphic is the account of the capture by Indians of the ship *Tonquin,* the massacre of all on board, and the subsequent explosion of the ship in which most of the Indians were killed.

Irving's heroes and adventurers, unlike those of most earlier American writers, are human. He likes them, and so does his reader. Irving could see the good not only in his namesake George Washington (who once, when Irving was an infant, patted his head and gave him a patriarchal blessing) but also in the fierce half-pirates and conquistadors of early Spanish America. He had a kind word to say for Aaron Burr after his trial and for Napoleon after Waterloo; he praised King Philip for his courage, his fidelity to his race, and his love of his family.

Perhaps Irving was able to understand his characters because he relied as much as possible on his own personal experiences in writing his stories of adventure. Not that Irving himself—despite his calmness when the ship on which he was voyaging was captured by Mediterranean pirates, despite his rambles through robber-infested Spain and his adventurous tour through the Shawnee and Osage country—was heroic. Far from it. In reality, he was a mild little man who dreaded even to give a speech in public—he broke down at the public dinner in New York for Dickens in 1842—and during his western trip was so unnerved when a false alarm of a Shawnee attack was made that he tangled himself in his trousers and could not get them on. He also studied locales and historical sources carefully. Much of the feeling of authenticity of the

SELIGMAN COLLECTION; MANUSCRIPT DIVISION, NEW YORK PUBLIC LIBRARY

Early in life Irving flirted with the idea of becoming an artist instead of a writer. That he had some talent for it is demonstrated by these sketches from his notebooks of 1805–6.

History of New York, for instance, was the result of Irving's thorough knowledge of the city gained from boyhood rambles about the streets and docks, as well as his meticulous research—Irving was one of the first to consult these records—into the old Dutch documents. If the strange adventure of Brom Bones and Ichabod Crane in Sleepy Hollow is vivid, it is partly because as a young man Irving had again and again visited the area. Similarly, the biography of Columbus was based in part on original research into long-neglected Spanish archives; Irving's intimate knowledge of Spain, where he lived from 1826 to 1829 and again (as United States minister) from 1842 to 1846, gave it added color. The western books, too, grew out of personal knowledge.

Irving's love for an adventurous past is at all times tempered with a nostalgic sadness that the beauty of old-time Spain and the heroism of the American frontier has yielded or is about to yield to the harsh commonplaces of modern existence. In the *History of New York,* for instance, he pictures the mythical Golden Age of the city before "Yankee" efficiency destroyed the comfortable Dutch phlegm. He liked to imagine, as he remarks in "The Legend of Sleepy Hollow," "a retreat whither I might steal from the world and its distractions, and dream quietly away the remnant of a troubled life." Perhaps the clearest statement of his nostalgia is in a little-known sketch, "The Creole Village," which was published in 1837. Here Irving, with very obvious criticism of the American civilization he sees around him, contrasts the calm, comfortable, peaceful, though poverty-stricken French Creole village in Louisiana with a bustling, speculating, ugly, businesslike "Yankee" town rising just down-river.

How many Americans must have sympathized with Irving's regret at the frenzied pace of "progress" and the change from old values to new! During his lifetime the territory of the nation as a whole at least tripled. His own beloved New York City multiplied more than ten times in population and changed from a friendly little provincial city into a hectic metropolis. Commerce and the industrial revolution swept away much of the calm old village life. The gentlemanly, almost feudal society of colonial New York changed, as James Fenimore Cooper so bitterly lamented in his trilogy of novels, *Satanstoe, The Chainbearer,* and *The Redskins,* to raw democracy. No wonder that Cooper fled either to Europe or, in imagination, to the depths of the wilderness with his frontiersman hero, Natty Bumppo—or that the poet William Cullen Bryant should seek the woods, where "calm shade" could "bring a kindred calm," and "the sweet breeze" could "waft a balm" to his "sick heart." But even beyond this general feeling of the time, Irving himself had perhaps even greater reason to dream fondly of the past. He had grown up in an atmosphere of comfort and security, had lived a gay, if somewhat spoiled life with the bright young literary group in New York, and had been indulged in his desire for a long, carefree trip through Europe. As a partner in his brothers' firm, he had had to do little but draw his income. But in 1818, as a result of debts incurred during the War of 1812, the business had failed. Irving found himself stranded in Europe, with little money and the sudden need to support himself. With courage and good humor he turned the writing that had been his avocation into his profession. He was not a man to complain. But perhaps, in a story like "Rip Van Winkle," when after twenty years' sleep old Rip returns to find his Dutch village changed almost beyond recognition, his old friends scattered, and the new inhabitants suspicious and quarrelsome, Irving is expressing a reaction to a personal situation as well as to the swift change in the nation.

Closely related to this nostalgia for the past is Irving's love of the picturesque. The moss-grown Creole village, the old Dutch farmhouses, the queer-gabled old mansions of New York appealed to him not only because they were old but because they made what he and his generation considered beautiful pictures. Irving always had a painter's eye. Indeed, on his visit to Europe in 1805 the well-known painter Washington Allston, recognizing his talent as a landscape artist, tried to persuade him to join the American art colony in Rome. And though Irving resisted the temptation to turn to canvas and brush, much of his literary technique relies on pictorial effects.

In "The Author's Account of Himself," prefixed to *The Sketch Book of Geoffrey Crayon* (Irving enjoyed a mild pun), he wrote of himself with his usual accuracy in self-criticism:

I have wandered through different countries, and witnessed many of the shifting scenes of life. I cannot say that I have studied them with the eye of the philosopher; but rather with the sauntering gaze with which humble lovers of the picturesque stroll from the window of one print-shop to another; caught, sometimes, by the delineations of beauty, sometimes by the distortions of caricature, and sometimes by the loveliness of landscape. As it is the fashion for modern tourists to travel pencil in hand, and bring home their portfolios filled with sketches, I am disposed to get up a few for the entertainment of my friends.

From the beginning Irving was a master of picturesque caricature in an age that delighted in it. Diedrich Knickerbocker's *History of New York,* for instance, presented a series of amusing scenes typical of Irving's peculiar brand of humor: Wouter Van Twil-

TEXT CONTINUED ON PAGE 92
A PORTFOLIO OF ILLUSTRATIONS CONTINUES ON THE FOLLOWING PAGES

AN ILLUSTRATED WASHINGTON IRVING MISCELLANY

COMPRISING
A SAVORY SALMAGUNDI
OF THE AUTHOR'S
MOST MEMORABLE PASSAGES
AS BROUGHT TO LIFE BY
A CENTURY OF ADMIRING ARTISTS

One of the qualities that has given Washington Irving a lasting reputation in American literature is his extraordinary ability to paint a picture with words, to evoke the sights and sounds and smells of spirited battles, peaceful landscapes, and the colorful legends of the past. His pages abound in passages of almost irresistible appeal to the artist. "You opened to me," the British painter C. R. Leslie wrote to him, "a new range of observation of my own art and a perception of the qualities and character of things . . ."

During Irving's own lifetime and in the century since his death, some of the best illustrators and painters both here and abroad have tried their hands at bringing to life pathetic old Rip Van Winkle and terrified young Ichabod Crane, at calling up the varied scenes of The Sketch Book, *or at re-creating the bountiful Christmases at Bracebridge Hall. On the next thirteen pages* AMERICAN HERITAGE *presents a portfolio of the work of these men, from F. O. C. Darley, the best known American illustrator of Irving's era, to Maxfield Parrish, N. C. Wyeth, and Arthur Rackham, of our own. With the reproductions are Irving's own descriptions, which remain astonishingly fresh.*

nests.... Then the Van Higginbottoms, of Wapping's creek. These came armed with ferules and birchen rods, being a race of schoolmasters... Then the Van Grolls, of Antony's Nose, who carried their liquor in fair round little pottles, by reason they could not bouse it out of their canteens, having such rare long noses. Then the Gardeniers, of Hudson and thereabouts, distinguished by many triumphant feats, such as robbing watermelon patches, smoking rabbits out

First of all came the Van Bummels, who . . . were short fat men, wearing exceeding large trunk-breeches, . . . the first inventors of suppawn, or mush and milk. Close in their rear marched the Van Vlotens, of Kaatskill, horrible quaffers of new cider, and arrant braggarts in their liquor. After them came the Van Pelts of Groodt Esopus, dexterous horsemen . . . mighty hunters of minks and musk-rats. . . . Then the Van Nests of Kinderhoeck, valiant robbers of bird's-

KNICKERBOCKER'S HISTORY OF NEW YORK

When in 1809 Irving published a satiric history of Dutch New York, he adopted the pseudonym "Diedrich Knickerbocker," described in press notices as "a small elderly gentleman, dressed in an old black coat and cocked hat" who had strangely disappeared, leaving behind a very curious manuscript. Irving, whose authorship was known almost immediately, hoped that his popular spoof would long be "thumbed and chuckled over by the family fireside." Spoof or not, passages like those quoted on these two pages—and illustrations like the ones shown with them—have given generations of readers their image of early New York. The sketch of Knickerbocker above is Darley's. Maxfield Parrish, 20th-century book, poster, and magazine artist, drew the Indian at left, whom Irving described as follows:

All the world knows the lamentable state in which these poor savages were found. Not only deficient in the comforts of life, but . . . blind to the miseries of their situation. But no sooner did the benevolent inhabitants of Europe behold their sad condition, than they immediately went to work to ameliorate and improve it. They introduced among them rum, gin, brandy, and the other comforts of life [and inspired] a thousand wants, of which they had before been ignorant. . . .

The fireplaces were of a truly patriarchal magnitude, where the whole family, old and young, master and servant, black and white, nay, even the very cat and dog, enjoyed a community of privilege. . . . Here the old burgher would sit in perfect silence, puffing his pipe, looking in the fire with half-shut eyes, and thinking of nothing for hours together; the goede vrouw . . . would employ herself diligently in spinning yarn, or knitting stockings. The young folks would crowd around [as] some old crone of a negro . . . would croak forth for a long winter afternoon a string of incredible stories about New-England witches . . . hair-breadth escapes, and bloody encounters among the Indians.

C. R. Leslie, Irving's great personal friend, drew the scene at right. George Cruikshank, Dickens' first illustrator, did the one below.

The sages . . . repaired to the council-chamber [where] . . . the governor, looking around for a moment with a lofty and soldier-like air, and resting one hand on the pommel of his sword, and flinging the other forth in a free and spirited manner, addressed them in a short but soul-stirring harangue.

To See the Big Parade, Lift Up These Pages

This colorful painting, entitled Peter Stuyvesant's Army Entering New Amsterdam, *is by an Irish genre artist named William Mulready. It illustrates Knickerbocker's parody of an actual event, Dutch mobilization in 1655 for the leisurely expedition—more like a picnic than a military campaign—against the forts held by the Swedes on the Delaware River.*

skill in shooting with the long bow. Then the Van Bunschotens, of Nyack and Kakiat, who . . . were gallant bushwhackers and hunters of raccoons. . . . Nothing could surpass the joy and martial pride of the lion-hearted Peter [extreme left, with peg leg] as he reviewed this mighty host of warriors, and he determined no longer to defer the gratification of his much-wished-for revenge upon the scoundrel Swedes at Fort Casimir.—*Knickerbocker's History of New York* of their holes, and the like, and by being great lovers of roasted pigs' tails. . . . Then the Van Hoesens, of Sing-Sing, great choristers and players upon the jews-harp. . . . Then the Couenhovens, of Sleepy Hollow. . . . a jolly race of publicans, who first discovered the magic artifice of conjuring a quart of wine into a pint bottle. Then the Van Kortlandts, who lived on the wild banks of the Croton, and were great killers of wild ducks, being much spoken of for their

WALTZ DANCE.

The Alhambra, Macmillan, 1896

The Court of Myrtles.

Washington Irving was a world traveler— and writer—of catholic tastes and interests. At top, superimposed on part of his manuscript of the five-volume Life of George Washington, *one of Irving's last works, is a wood engraving by Alexander Anderson for* Salmagundi, *one of his first. Below these is a drawing by W. F. Wilson for* The Adventures of Captain Bonneville, U.S.A., *a pioneering history which helped stimulate America's interest in its western heroes. One of the delightful products of Irving's Spanish sojourns was* The Alhambra, *for which Joseph Pennell made nearly 300 sketches; one is seen at right. But to many readers the tales of Dutch life in "the ancient cities of the Manhattoes"—which inspired not only illustrators but painters like John Quidor (opposite page)—will always represent Irving at the top of his form.*

The Alhambra . . . was the royal abode of the Moorish kings, where, surrounded with the splendors and refinements of Asiatic luxury, they held dominion over . . . a terrestrial paradise, and made their last stand for empire in Spain. . . . Externally it is a rude congregation of towers and battlements . . . giving little promise of the grace and beauty which prevail within. —*The Alhambra*

BROOKLYN MUSEUM

Wolfert lay on his back . . . his whole visage the picture of death. He begged the lawyer to be brief, for he felt his end approaching. . . . "I give and bequeath," said Wolfert faintly, "my small farm"—

"What—all!" exclaimed the lawyer. . . . "All that great patch of land with cabbages and sun-flowers, which the corporation is just going to run a main street through?"

"The same," said Wolfert, with a heavy sigh. . . .

"I wish him joy that inherits it!" said the little lawyer, chuckling, and rubbing his hands involuntarily. . . . "He'll be one of the richest men in the place. . . ."

The expiring Wolfert seemed to step back from the threshold of existence: his eyes again lighted up . . . "Say you so?" cried Wolfert, half thrusting one leg out of bed, "Why then I think I'll not make my will yet!"

—*"Wolfert Webber," from* Tales of a Traveller

The Legend of Sleepy Hollow

On a fine autumnal afternoon, Ichabod, in a pensive mood, sat enthroned on the lofty stool . . . In his hand he swayed a ferule, that sceptre of despotic power; the birch of justice reposed on three nails . . . while on the desk before him might be seen sundry . . . prohibited weapons, detected upon the persons of idle urchins; such as half-munched apples, popguns . . . and . . . little paper gamecocks.

Schoolmaster Crane and charges were drawn by Darley. The courting scene below is by the painter Daniel Huntington, a student of Morse's.

Katrina Van Tassel, the daughter and only child of a substantial Dutch farmer . . . was a blooming lass of fresh eighteen; plump as a partridge; ripe and melting and rosy-cheeked [and] universally famed, not merely for her beauty, but her vast expectations. She was withal a little of a coquette . . . She wore . . . a provokingly short petticoat, to display the prettiest foot and ankle in the country around. Ichabod Crane had a soft and foolish heart toward the sex; and [it was no wonder that] so tempting a morsel soon found favor in his eyes.

VOSE GALLERIES OF BOSTON, INC.

"If I can but reach that bridge," thought Ichabod, "I am safe." Just then he heard the black steed panting and blowing close behind him; he even fancied that he felt his hot breath. Another convulsive kick in the ribs, and old Gunpowder sprang upon the bridge; he thundered over the resounding planks; he gained the opposite side; and now Ichabod cast a look behind to see if his pursuer should vanish, according to the rule, in a flash of fire and brimstone. Just then he saw the goblin rising in his stirrups, and in the very act of hurling his head at him.

G. W. A. Jenkinson's version of the famous scene in which Brom Bones, posing as the "headless horseman," puts to flight his rival for Katrina's hand.

Rip Van Winkle

IRVING

NATIONAL GALLERY OF ART (MELLON COLLECTION)

The appearance of Rip, with his long, grizzled beard, his rusty fowling-piece, his uncouth dress, and an army of women and children at his heels, soon attracted the attention of the tavern-politicians. They crowded round him, eyeing him from head to foot with great curiosity. . . . a knowing, self-important old gentleman, in a sharp cocked hat, made his way through the crowd . . . and planting himself before Van Winkle, with one arm akimbo, the other resting on his cane . . . demanded who he was, and what was his name. "God knows," exclaimed he, at his wit's end; "I'm not myself—I'm somebody else—that's me yonder—no—that's somebody else got into my shoes [in fact, the lad is his son]—I was myself last night, but I fell asleep on the mountain, and they've changed my gun, and everything's changed, and I'm changed, and I can't tell what's my name, or who I am!"

Quidor exhibited The Return of Rip Van Winkle *(left) at the National Academy in 1829. Besides the two in this portfolio, he painted fifteen other Irving scenes. The gnomes of Rip's dream (right) were seen quite differently by two illustrators, N. C. Wyeth (top) and Arthur Rackham.*

Passing through the ravine, they came to a hollow, like a small amphitheater, surrounded by perpendicular precipices, over the brinks of which impending trees shot their branches . . . On a level spot in the center was a company of odd-looking personages playing at ninepins. They were dressed in a quaint, outlandish fashion; some wore short doublets, others jerkins, with long knives in their belts, and most of them had enormous breeches. . . . Their visages, too, were peculiar: one had a large beard, broad face, and small piggish eyes; the face of another seemed to consist entirely of nose. . . . There was one who seemed to be the commander . . . a stout old gentleman, with a weather-beaten countenance; he wore a laced doublet, broad belt and hanger, high crowned hat and feather, red stockings, and high-heeled shoes . . . Though . . . evidently amusing themselves, yet they maintained the gravest faces, the most mysterious silence.

OLD · CHRISTMAS

Americans of Irving's time, whose own traditions had no patina of age, often idealized those of the mother country. Of no tradition was this truer than of the bounteous Christmases in England's great manor houses, celebrated by Irving in The Sketch Book. *The essays, later published as* Old Christmas, *were illustrated by English artists like Cecil Aldin—five of whose drawings appear here—in the same graceful style that makes Irving's own prose a pleasure to read and read again.*

I had scarcely got into bed when a strain of music seemed to break forth in the air just below the window. I listened, and found it proceeded from a band, which I concluded to be the waits from some neighboring village. They went round the house, playing under the windows. I drew aside the curtains to hear them more distinctly. The moonbeams fell through the upper part of the casement, partially lighting up the antiquated apartment. The sounds, as they receded, became more soft and aerial, and seemed to accord with the quiet and moonlight. I listened and listened—they became more and more tender and remote, and, as they gradually died away, my head sunk upon the pillow, and I fell asleep.

The dinner was served up in the great hall, where the Squire always held his Christmas banquet. A blazing, crackling fire of logs had been heaped on to warm the spacious apartment, and the flame went sparkling and wreathing up the wide-mouthed chimney. . . . We were ushered into this banqueting scene with the sound of minstrelsy, the old harper being seated on a stool beside the fireplace . . . twanging his instrument.

Master Simon . . . was a tight brisk little man . . . with a drollery and lurking waggery of expression that was irresistible. He was evidently the wit of the family . . . the idol of the younger part of the company, who laughed at everything he said or did.

If you mean to be a historical figure, it is a good idea to get in touch with a leading literary figure—a Longfellow, a Homer, a Vergil. Paul Revere, Odysseus, Aeneas—they all took this precaution. Poor Captain Jack Jouett didn't. And as a result this six-foot-four, two-hundred-pound giant from Virginia, who saved the leaders of the American Revolution from a disheartening and possibly disastrous reverse, has been left out of practically all the history books.

His forty-mile ride from Cuckoo Tavern to Monticello was one of the significant minor exploits of the struggle for independence. Unfortunately, it lacks a chronicler of adequate stature. Henry Wadsworth Longfellow, God rest his bones, put Revere on the map. He even gave us the exact hour at which Paul reached Concord on his "midnight ride," despite the fact that Revere himself says he was captured by the British before he got there. Jack Jouett's far longer and more perilous nocturnal dash across the Virginia countryside sorely needs a rousing ballad, preferably accurate as to facts, but comparable in popular appeal to the famous "Paul Revere's Ride."

JACK JOUETT'S RIDE

His feat was more daring than Paul Revere's, but Virginia's hero had, alas, no Longfellow

By VIRGINIUS DABNEY

Jouett's epochal exploit took place on the night of June 3–4, 1781, when the fortunes of the American colonists appeared far from prosperous. The traitor Benedict Arnold, by that time a British general, had been raiding and pillaging along the James from the river's mouth to Richmond, the Old Dominion's capital. General Cornwallis had detached his "hunting leopard," Lieutenant Colonel Banastre Tarleton, with 180 dragoons and 70 mounted infantrymen, to make a surprise march to Charlottesville, where the Virginia legislature was meeting following its flight from Richmond. His object was to capture Thomas Jefferson, author of that seditious document, the Declaration of Independence, and now governor of Virginia; Patrick Henry, whose "Give me liberty or give me death!" had sounded the call to arms six years before; and these signers of the Declaration: Richard Henry Lee, whose resolutions introduced in the Continental Congress in 1776 had led to adoption of the Declaration; Benjamin Harrison, ancestor of two future Presidents; and Thomas Nelson, Jr., who had urged armed resistance to Great Britain in 1775 and had spent most of his fortune equipping soldiers for the Continental Army.

Tarleton's raid was as secret as he knew how to make it. He planned to cover the last seventy miles in twenty-four hours—an eighteenth-century blitzkrieg—and to pounce on Jefferson and the assemblymen unexpectedly. Valuable stores also were to be seized.

The British—many of whom were riding blooded horses seized on Virginia plantations—reached Cuckoo Tavern, Louisa County, between nine and ten o'clock on the evening of June 3. Up to that point, their movements had been successfully masked.

Here Jouett enters the picture. This twenty-seven-year-old native of Albemarle County was a captain in the Virginia militia, as were his three brothers, one of whom had been killed at Brandywine. Before the Revolution, the John Jouetts, father and son, had signed the Albemarle Declaration, whereby 202 residents of the county renounced allegiance to King George. And during the war, records show, "Commissary" John Jouett, Sr., sold considerable beef and other needed supplies from his Louisa County farm to the quartermasters of the Continental Army.

Jack Jouett may have been at or near Cuckoo Tavern on the night of June 3 while attending to his father's interests in that vicinity. At all events, Thomas Jefferson wrote years after, the young militiaman saw the British dragoons "pass his father's house" in Louisa, and immediately suspected their object.

It was about ten o'clock. At once Captain Jouett leapt upon his thoroughbred, resolved to dash for Monticello and Charlottesville to warn the Assembly. He was forced to use a seldom-traveled route, for the British were on the main highway. Even the best roads of that era, with their ruts, mudholes, and thank-you-ma'ams, would be considered virtually impassable today; the difficulties that confronted this lone horseman on his all-night ride over backwoods byways can only be imagined.

The distance from Cuckoo Tavern to Charlottesville is about forty miles. The terrain, embracing parts of Louisa and Albemarle counties, is rolling and hilly. (It is in Louisa that the traveler from Tidewater first glimpses, on the far side of Albemarle, the soft contours of the Blue Ridge Mountains.) The moon was nearly full that night, but we do not know whether clouds obscured it. Even in bright moonlight, Jack Jouett was risking serious if not fatal injury in using this almost pathless route. As he rode through the woods and undergrowth of a virtual wilderness, his face was cruelly lashed and scarred.

Meanwhile Tarleton, by his own account, halted his troopers at 11 P.M. on a plantation near Louisa Courthouse. After resting for three hours, they set out again at 2 A.M. Not long thereafter they encountered a train of eleven wagons loaded with arms and clothing for Gen. Nathanael Greene's Continental troops in South Carolina. They burned the wagon train instead of taking it with them, Tarleton wrote, in order that no time might be lost.

Soon after daybreak, the expedition reached Castle Hill, home of the celebrated Dr. Thomas Walker, the explorer, and nearby Belvoir, home of his son, John. "Some of the principal gentlemen of Virginia . . . were taken out of their beds," Tarleton wrote. "Part were paroled . . . while others were carried off." There was a "halt of half an hour" to refresh the horses, he added, after which the troops moved on toward Charlottesville.

Various legends have grown up around this halt at Castle Hill. The principal one says that Dr. Walker craftily offered Tarleton an elaborate breakfast, the consumption of which so delayed the Briton that Jack Jouett was able to beat him to Monticello and Charlottesville. Another legend has British dragoons stealing, one after the other, two breakfasts which had been prepared for their commander and Dr. Walker telling Tarleton that he would have to post a guard on the kitchen if he desired nourishment. This was done, the story continues, and the cook and attendant flunkies finally served the third breakfast to the Colonel intact. But by the time he had eaten it, Jefferson and most of the legislature had escaped. There are even some ridiculous references in one modern account to "potent mint juleps, Sally Lunn and waffles."

If breakfast *was* consumed at Castle Hill by any Briton in the early morning of June 4, 1781, we may be reasonably sure that there was no such menu as this.

ILLUSTRATED FOR AMERICAN HERITAGE BY BLAKE HAMPTON

"[He] saw the British . . . and suspected their object."

Aside from the fact that juleps and other such sybaritic provender at so early an hour seem absurd under the circumstances, Tarleton would hardly have been stupid enough to fall into so obvious a trap. His own statement that he halted only half an hour at Castle Hill to rest his horses impresses one as far more authentic, although in his account he may have shortened the actual time somewhat in order not to appear lacking in zeal.

While Tarleton and his men were tarrying at Castle Hill, Jouett was riding through the dawn toward Monticello. His route took him to the Rivanna River ford at the hamlet of Milton. A few miles farther on, he made the ascent to Jefferson's stately mansion, arriving at about 4:30 A.M., several hours ahead of the British; their relatively brief halt at the Walker estate cannot have been responsible for their failure to bag Jefferson and the other patriots.

On reaching Monticello, Jouett proceeded at once to rouse the sleeping occupants. Among them, besides Jefferson, were the Speakers and other members of the two houses of the General Assembly. Jefferson not only thanked Jouett for his timely warning but is understood to have tendered a bracing glass or two of his best Madeira. Refreshed, the rider mounted his horse and rode the remaining two miles to Charlottesville, where he awakened dozens more of the snoring solons.

Jefferson and his guests had been far from panic-stricken by the tidings. They "breakfasted at leisure," Jefferson afterward wrote; then the guests joined their colleagues in town. Jefferson, remaining behind at Monticello, made arrangements to send his wife and children to Enniscorthy, the Coles estate fourteen miles distant, via Blenheim, the Carter estate. He then spent nearly two hours securing his important papers.

Suddenly Captain Christopher Hudson, en route to join Lafayette's forces, arrived at a gallop to say that British troopers were ascending the mountain to Monticello. Jefferson sent his family off at once in their carriage but was himself in no great hurry to depart. He tied his horse at a point on the road between Monticello and Carter's Mountain, and through his telescope scanned the Charlottesville streets. Seeing no signs of unwonted activity, and hearing no approaching hoofbeats on the mountainside, he started back to Monticello for a few last-minute arrangements. He soon noticed, however, that he had dropped his light "walking sword," and returned to pick it up. He focused his telescope for a final look toward the town and was startled to see British dragoons, in their green uniforms faced with white, and mounted infantrymen, wearing red, swarming in the streets.

Instantly Jefferson leaped upon his horse and plunged into the woods. The British were already at Monticello: he had made the narrowest sort of escape. He eluded Tarleton's men, and joined his family later in the day for dinner at Blenheim.

Tarleton himself did not go to Monticello but remained in Charlottesville. He gave strict orders to Captain McLeod, commander of the detachment he was sending to capture Jefferson, not to damage the house in any way. An account handed down in the family, and accepted by Henry S. Randall, Jefferson's mid-nineteenth-century biographer, has it that when the British suddenly hove into view on the mountaintop, Martin, Jefferson's Negro body servant, was passing silver and other articles to Caesar, another slave, through a trap door in the wooden floor of the portico. As the dragoons burst upon the scene, Martin dropped the trap door, leaving Caesar in total darkness. He remained there, quiet and uncomplaining, until the raiders left some eighteen hours later. Apparently they need not have feared: except for the pilferage of a few articles in the cellar, McLeod's men carried out their instructions.

By contrast, the main body of General Cornwallis' army, which Tarleton joined next day at Elk Hill, Jefferson's plantation at Point of Fork (now Columbia), wrought devastation far and wide. Not content with burning the barns, destroying the crops, taking the horses and cattle, and cutting the throats of the young colts, Cornwallis even carried off thirty Negroes. He herded them in with other slaves who were suffering from smallpox and "putrid fever," and most of them died.

In Charlottesville, meanwhile, the General Assembly was hurriedly taking its departure. The members had convened hastily on getting the word from Jouett that the British were coming and had adjourned at once, resolving to meet three days later at Staunton, forty miles to the west beyond the mountains.

Tarleton was so close on their heels that although Patrick Henry, Richard Henry Lee, Benjamin Harrison, Thomas Nelson, Jr., and numerous others got away, seven assemblymen were taken. One who managed to escape was General Edward Stevens, who was recuperating from a wound received at the Battle of Guilford Courthouse. Randall relates that Stevens was plainly dressed and mounted on a shabby horse, whereas Jack Jouett, riding his thoroughbred, was dressed in "a scarlet coat and military hat and plume," for he "had an eccentric custom of wearing such habiliments." The British ignored Stevens, thinking he was a person of no importance, and went after Jouett, whose dress led them to believe him an officer of high rank. But the athletic, well-mounted Jouett was too fast for them, and made his getaway. General Stevens, meanwhile, had taken advantage of the diversion to disappear.

"Tarleton ... planned ... to pounce on Jefferson."

Thomas Jefferson's political opponents inside and outside the state tried to make it appear that he had behaved in a cowardly fashion at the time of Tarleton's raid. For many years thereafter his perennial enemies, the Federalists, sought to picture him as having fled ignominiously before the British. Tarleton himself wrote that Jefferson "provided for his personal safety with a precipitate retreat."

All this was grossly unfair. If anything, Jefferson waited too long at Monticello after being warned by Jouett, with the result that he barely escaped capture. Certainly he is no more to be criticized than the legislators, who beat a more "precipitate retreat" than he. As a matter of fact, when a group of them—including Henry, Harrison, and John Tyler, Sr.—stopped in a hut beyond Charlottesville, the old woman of the house proceeded to abuse them roundly for "running away." But when she found that Henry was one of their number, she apologized.

What would have been the fate of such men as Jefferson, Henry, Harrison, Nelson, and Lee, if they had fallen into British hands? They would almost certainly

58

have been carried off into captivity by Tarleton—just as he carried off several "gentlemen" taken at or near Castle Hill on the previous day; it is hardly conceivable that men of the stature of Jefferson, Henry, and the rest would have been paroled. Their capture would have been a serious blow to the morale of the Continentals, especially at a time when things were going rather badly for their cause. Incalculable, even catastrophic, results might have followed from such a coup.

The General Assembly of Virginia was deeply sensible of its debt to Jack Jouett, for a few days afterward, on June 15, it adopted the following resolution:

Resolved: That the executive be desired to present to Captain John Jouett an elegant sword and pair of pistols as a memorial of the high sense which the General Assembly entertain of his activity and enterprise in watching the motions of the enemy's cavalry on their late incursion to Charlottesville and conveying to the assembly timely information of their approach, whereby the designs of the enemy were frustrated and many valuable stores preserved.

Jouett was given the pistols in 1783, but it was twenty years before he received the "elegant sword." By that time he had made quite a name for himself beyond the Alleghenies, in present-day Kentucky.

His career there started out badly. According to a story handed down in the family, he and his companions were moving westward through the Cumberland Gap and along Daniel Boone's Wilderness Road when they heard the cries of a woman coming from a lonely cabin. On investigating, they found a man beating his wife. Jouett went gallantly to the lady's rescue and knocked her husband down. But the Virginian discovered at once that he who intervenes in such an intramural dispute incurs the wrath of both parties thereto: the lady reached for a long-handled frying pan and hit Jouett over the head so forcefully that the bottom of the pan was knocked out and the rim driven down around his neck. Not until he found a blacksmith, thirty-five miles down the road, was he able to disengage his head.

Undiscouraged, Jouett settled down in Mercer County and entered politics. He helped Kentucky break off from Virginia and become a sovereign state, served four terms in the new legislature, pioneered livestock breeding in Woodford County—in the bluegrass where today great racing stables raise swift colts for the Derby—and in his later years was the friend of Andrew Jackson, Henry Clay, and the great families of his adopted state. Among his numerous children was one of America's most noted portrait painters, Matthew Harris Jouett ("I sent Matthew to college to make a gentleman of him," said old Jack, "and he has turned out to be nothing but a damned sign painter"). And among Matthew's children was James Edward "Fighting Jim" Jouett, a distinguished naval officer, who seems to have shared his grandfather's fate in being forgotten by history. What Admiral Farragut reportedly said at the Battle of Mobile Bay was: "Damn the torpedoes! Four bells! Captain Drayton go ahead! Jouett full speed!" Alas, it is usually remembered by the average schoolboy as "Damn the torpedoes! Full speed ahead!"

By the time "Fighting Jim's" hour of glory struck, his grandfather was of course long since dead. And by the world forgotten: he was buried in the family cemetery at his Bath County farm, Peeled Oak, but the grave was unmarked, and it took a twentieth-century researcher, the late Mrs. Joel M. Cochran of Charlottesville, Virginia, to find the spot where the old Revolutionary hero was laid to rest.

Yes, Jack Jouett's ride from Cuckoo Tavern to Monticello cries out for a ballad that will seize the fancy of the American people. The hoofbeats of his steed, toiling and sweating through the warm June night across forty miles of Virginia countryside, come echoing down the years. Jack Jouett gave some of America's greatest patriots a timely warning in one of the Revolution's dark hours, but his valorous deed has been well-nigh forgotten. He deserves a kinder fate.

"*. . . Jouett was riding through the dawn to Monticello.*"

For the past twenty-five years Virginius Dabney has been editor of the Richmond Times-Dispatch. *A winner of the Pulitzer prize for editorial writing, he is the author of several books and articles about America's past, is currently vice president of the Virginia Historical Society, and is chairman of its publications committee.*

Dartmouth was a missionary school in the New Hampshire wilderness when John Ledyard entered in 1772. He stayed only a year, then left for good in a homemade dugout canoe. The 1793 print shown here is the earliest known view of the college.

Captain Cook's American

By E. M. HALLIDAY

Connecticut-born John Ledyard became the first American to see Alaska and Hawaii. Years before Lewis and Clark, he planned to cross the North American continent—from west to east

From Hanover to Haapai

Taking to the sea, Ledyard in 1776 joined Captain James Cook in his search for a Pacific outlet to the fabled Northwest Passage. On one Polynesian island, Haapai in the Friendlys, Cook's party was entertained (above) by native gladiators.

If a judicious fate had deliberately selected one American as the first of his countrymen to see Alaska and Hawaii, our future forty-ninth and fiftieth states—to represent America to them, and them to America—it could hardly have chosen better than in John Ledyard of Connecticut. He was a man who seemed to have bred into his very bones an intuitive grasp of those American ideals which his friend Thomas Jefferson so enduringly expressed in the Declaration of Independence. To Ledyard nothing appeared more self-evident than that all men, of whatever race, color, or creed, were created equal, and that their common heritage was the free pursuit of life, liberty, and happiness. Primitive people could sense in him a direct and simple faith that human beings were indeed all of one family; and accordingly, whether they were Polynesians or Aleuts, they treated him like a brother.

Ledyard's upbringing in the provincial democracy that was pre-Revolutionary New England, with an intellectual background colored by the European Enlightenment, no doubt encouraged his attitudes; yet to a great extent they must have been his by nature. Born in Groton, Connecticut, in November, 1751, he was the son of a sea captain engaged in the West Indies trade. There could have been no lack of adventure tales and cosmopolitan atmosphere for John in his early boyhood. But his father died at sea when John was only eleven, and the lad soon went to live in his grandfather's house at Hartford. It was a conservative ménage, and young John fitted it poorly: he was too much inclined to go without his hat, wear his shirt unbuttoned at the neck, and take a close interest in tramps and wandering Indians.

During his teens John Ledyard vacillated between a career in law and one in the ministry. When he was twenty, a friend of his grandfather's, Dr. Eleazar Wheelock, intervened. Wheelock, who had founded at Hanover, New Hampshire, a combination college and training school for missionaries to the Indians, asked if John would like to come up to help in the good work and at the

John Ledyard, a reconstructed portrait

61

This view of Tahiti was painted by William Hodges, a member of an earlier Cook expedition to the Pacific. While Hodges' landscape was accurate, his natives, at lower right, were patterned after the eighteenth-century ideal of the noble savage.

same time secure a college education. Since there seemed nothing better to do at the moment, he packed his few belongings, and in April, 1772, left for the rustic environs of Dartmouth College.

Although Ledyard's sojourn at Dartmouth was not long, it is possible that he left a stamp upon it almost as deep as that of the Reverend Dr. Wheelock. Broad-shouldered, yellow-haired, and handsome, the new student had a generous good humor that attracted his classmates even though they found him a bit eccentric in taste and manner. He was charged with energy; things were never dull when Ledyard was around. He is credited with having introduced dramatics into the extracurricular activities, delighting his fellow students with a sensational performance in Addison's *Cato*. Better, he unofficially founded the Dartmouth Outing Club by inveigling a few undergraduates into an overnight camping trip in the snowdrifts of a nearby mountain.

But the most important thing he did, in view of his later career, was to vanish into the north woods for three months of travel and visitation among the Iroquois Indians. Christian proselytizing was his excuse, but there was no evidence that he converted any of the red men. On the contrary, the conversion may be said to have gone the other way. For Ledyard was fascinated by the customs and attitudes of this primitive culture and found himself with no disposition to alter or improve.

When he returned from the land of the Iroquois in the spring of 1773, Ledyard was more restless than ever. Having become entangled with Dr. Wheelock over payment of college bills, he decided to take a bold way out of his troubles. Evidently he had picked up some knowledge of dugouts from the Indians, and with the help of a few classmates he proceeded to hew out a large canoe from a pine tree cut on the bank of the Connecticut River. Near the end of April, with a fresh New England spring greening the New Hampshire woods, Ledyard equipped himself with a bearskin robe, some smoked venison, and a couple of books, and set out on his first voyage. It seemed a gallant gesture, a fine blow struck against humdrum reality, and it left an indelible impression on Dartmouth College. The undergraduates who still celebrate his feat each year by canoeing down the Connecticut to Hartford generally return to Dartmouth,

Tahiti: the Image of Eden

In another Hodges painting, Tahitian fighting-galleys parade their strength for the explorers. Though most Europeans saw the island as a primitive Arcadia, war was not unknown to it, nor (as Ledyard noted) were cannibalism and infanticide.

satisfied with the gesture. But John Ledyard never went back.

Before another year was out, Ledyard had crossed the Atlantic twice, and had discovered himself to be quite at ease in his father's calling. He was not so devoted to it, however, that other lures were unfelt. When his ship, a trading vessel, touched at Gibraltar in 1774, he turned up missing one morning. The ship's captain, an old friend of Ledyard's father, made a search and found John, resplendent in a red coat, drilling with the British garrison. The captain talked the commander into releasing his new recruit, and Ledyard, with some reluctance, returned to the ship.

He was to get his red coat again, ironically enough, just before his native country declared its independence. The fourth of July, 1776, found Ledyard on the deck of H.M.S. *Resolution* as it lay off Plymouth, England, about to sail for the Cape of Good Hope and the Pacific. Knowing little of the stirring events back home, he had eagerly signed up with Captain James Cook in the spring of 1776 when fortune had brought him to London. Cook was no doubt impressed with the young American's bursting good health, good looks, and alert enthusiasm; at any rate he saw to it that Ledyard was commissioned a corporal in the complement of marines chosen to go along with a hand-picked crew.

It was to be the third of Captain Cook's momentous voyages of discovery in the Pacific. Few men in history have so changed the map of the world as this sailor son of a Yorkshire farmer. A near-genius in marine cartography, he had already made notable surveys of the St. Lawrence River and the coasts of Labrador and Newfoundland before the Admiralty, in 1768, sent him on his first mission to the South Seas. Like images emerging on a photographic print thrust into developing fluid, Australia and New Zealand took shape on the map as Cook cruised and charted their shores. Going out again in 1772, he penetrated the Antarctic Circle and proved that the old rumor of a great continent lying just south of Australia was a myth; he partially made up for this erasure by discovering New Caledonia and a few smaller islands.

But the North Pacific was still largely a realm of wild surmise. The exploration of this vast area and, more specifically, one last search for a Northwest Passage connecting the Atlantic and the Pacific, were the goals of Cook's third voyage. The dream of easy access

63

Cook's ships, the Resolution *and the* Discovery, *made their first landing in Hawaii on the island of Kauai (above). The natives, who had never seen white men before, were, Ledyard reported, "inexpressibly surprized, though not intimidated."*

to China across the top of the American continent—perhaps by a strait linking Hudson Bay to the Pacific—was one that died hard in the minds of English kings, queens, and navigators. Sailing from the south, Sir Francis Drake had tried to make it a reality for Queen Elizabeth in 1579, but never got farther than what is now the state of Washington; many others had tried, in later years, from the northeast. Cook's aim—kept secret from his crew until they had been gone from England for many months—was to strike the western shore of North America at approximately the forty-ninth parallel of latitude—which passes through Vancouver Island off the mainland of present-day British Columbia—and then nose carefully up the coastline, charting as he went, and poking into any likely-looking inlet that might conceivably be the Passage. At best, he would get through; at worst, it was hoped, he would contribute some realistic zigs and zags to the map of northwestern North America, the eighteenth-century outline of which was absurdly smooth.

Cook was in his prime as a sea captain—he was forty-seven in 1776—and knew all there was to learn about successfully conducting a long ocean voyage in a sailing ship. His qualifications as surveyor and navigator were matched by a shrewd insight into the nature of the British seaman; he was always firm but seldom unjust, and made the men feel a rare sense of participation in the mission of each voyage. In an age when it was common to lose nearly half a ship's company through disease on a long expedition, Cook had no peer as a guardian of his crews' lives and health. He seemed to have a sixth sense about such shipboard scourges as dysentery and scurvy: his innovations in diet and sanitation alone would have earned him a place of honor in the annals of the sea. Of 117 men who sailed on the *Resolution,* only five succumbed to sickness on a voyage lasting over four years; her consort ship, the *Discovery,* lost not a single man.

Although only a corporal, John Ledyard ranked as an officer in Cook's company, and as such found himself among an extraordinary group of men. There was George Vancouver, a midshipman who later (1792–95) would immortalize his own name by leading a similar exploratory venture. There was Lieutenant John Gore, one of the most experienced sailors afloat—born a Virginian, but a veteran of the Royal Navy for so many years that he no longer considered himself a colonial.

The Discovery of Hawaii

The Hawaiians treated Cook like a god. At one ceremony, painted by shipboard artist John Webber, priests draped the explorer (center) in a red cloth and sacrificed a pig in his honor. Earlier they had offered him a roasted human arm.

And there was the sailing master, William Bligh, who because of the mutiny led by Fletcher Christian was fated to achieve a most unsavory reputation as captain of the *Bounty*, but who nevertheless was a first-rate navigator and deck officer. Besides these accomplished seamen there was a parcel of scientists who interested Ledyard even more: an astronomer, a botanist, and an artist sent along to record flora and fauna, including Polynesian natives.

One Polynesian native was already on the *Resolution*. This was Omai, a young man from Raïatéa (an island near Tahiti) adopted on Cook's second voyage and taken to London. Having soon acquired a gloss of fashionable manners and upper-class English speech, he was the guest most in demand at London parties for an entire season—arrayed not in his native loincloth, but in silk, velvet, and lace. It was the era of the "noble savage," that sentimental invention of eighteenth-century Europe which was to find its American counterpart in the saga of Hiawatha. Almost everyone in London society saw Omai as Nature's original gentleman; even Dr. Samuel Johnson, no romanticist, remarked that his table manners were unimpeachable.

Ledyard, observing Omai at close quarters as the *Resolution* carried them toward the South Pacific, was not favorably impressed. As a result of his experience with Indians he had already formed the opinion that it was a mistake to transplant a native from his own culture to that of "civilization," and in Omai he saw not only signs of corruption but evidence of defects in the original specimen. "His ignorance and vanity," Ledyard noted in his journal, "are insupportable." Soon he was to see natives who struck him as much finer representatives of Polynesian culture, both physically and mentally.

A splendid example was Phenow, a young chief of the Tonga Islands, where Cook (who called them the Friendly Islands) visited in the spring of 1777. This tall statuesque youth Ledyard described as "one of the most graceful men I ever saw in the Pacific ocean. He was open and free in his disposition, full of vivacity, enterprising and bold . . . the idol of the fair, having himself one of the most beautiful brunetts for a wife, that the hands of nature ever finished."

That quick switch of attention to the female is a ready clue to what Ledyard, like so many others, found almost overwhelmingly attractive about Polynesia. If Omai was a fraud of sorts, there was nothing false

65

A French panoramic wallpaper depicting places visited by Captain Cook during his Pacific voyages was designed by J. C. Charvet in 1804–5. According to a contemporary brochure, the decoration attempted to create "a community of taste and enjoyment between those who live in a state of civilization and those who are at the outset of

the use of their native intelligence." From the left, the scenes show Nootka Indians drying fish; a bucolic group of Friendly Islanders; musicians playing drums and nose flutes; dancing girls performing for O-too, king of Tahiti; and, at far right, the armed clash (shown in middle distance) in which Cook was killed in February, 1779.

PHILADELPHIA MUSEUM OF ART

Cook's ships probed the Pacific coast of North America from the forty-ninth parallel to the Arctic Ocean in the hope of finding a Northwest Passage. Here, longboats investigating Prince William Sound on the Gulf of Alaska are met by Indian bidarkas.

about the beauty of the brown-skinned, marvelous girls who swam out to the ships with breasts entrancingly bare, their white teeth flashing in superb contrast to their black hair whenever—and it seemed to be always—they smiled.

The whole company was dazzled. Even Captain Cook, a man of severe views, was moved to eulogize the charms of Polynesian women, and his officers were ecstatic. "Their natural complexion," one wrote, "is that kind of clear olive or *Brunette,* which many people in Europe prefer to the finest white and red . . . the skin is most delicately smooth and soft. . . . Their eyes, especially those of the women, are full of expression, sometimes sparkling with fire, and sometimes melting with softness; their teeth also are, almost without exception, most beautifully even and white, and their breath perfectly without taint."

Ledyard took meticulous notes on the natives of the Tongas. He described every detail he could of this exotic environment, and always with an effort to restrain his natural enthusiasm for the sake of accurate observation. As full of ebullient life as the islanders themselves, he sometimes found it hard to maintain a scientific attitude, especially since the natives seemed to be attracted to him as much as he was to them. But he worked at it. Their food, their clothing, their implements and weapons, their language, their religion, their songs and dances—remarks on everything went into his journal, along with thoughtful speculation as to the origins of Polynesian culture. He avoided sentimentalizing the South Sea Islands as Paradise regained, soberly considering such shadows amid the romance as human sacrifice and infanticide.

Midsummer of 1777 found the *Resolution* and the *Discovery* at Tahiti. The Tongas had offered persuasive erotic temptations, but those of Tahiti were irresistible. Although upper-class Tahitian ladies were not without reserve, the ordinary young women of the island were so eager to grant what Cook called "personal favours" to the visitors that everyone who had not been there before was incredulous. What was most surprising was their utter lack of shame—so far removed from depravity, however, that to Ledyard it appeared a kind of original innocence. The sailors, by no means loath, were yet hardly prepared by their background to adjust to companions who, as one Englishman observed, "gratify every appetite and passion

Vain Search for a Northwest Passage

When Cook first touched North America at Nootka Sound—one of many inlets that failed to reveal the elusive Passage—a homesick Ledyard wrote: "Though more than 2,000 miles from the nearest part of New-England I felt myself plainly affected."

before witnesses with no more sense of impropriety than we feel when we satisfy our hunger at a social board with our family or friends." (At the same time, Captain Cook could record the following puzzled entry in his journal: ". . . the women never upon any account eat with the men but always by themselves. What can be the reason of so unusual a Custom it is hard to say . . . ; they were often asked the reason but never gave no other answer but that they did it because it was right.")

As for Ledyard, he is reticent about his own experiences in Tahiti; but certainly there is a note of intense personal feeling in a remark he makes about the island love affair of one of his crewmates: "Love like this is not to be found in those countries where the boasted refinements of sentiment too often circumscribe the purity of affection and narrow it away to mere conjugal fidelity." He left Tahiti with his hands tattooed in the native style—a practice, as he tells us, among some of the men who fell in love with island girls and wished to make a ceremonial exchange of tokens.

Near the end of 1777 Cook decided that it was time to tear his crew from the delights of the South Pacific and push northward into the unknown ocean above the equator. They encountered nothing but a few coral reefs until early in January, 1778; then a stir of excitement arose as signs of land began to occur. A tree branch drifted by; small birds flew past. At daybreak on January 18, the lookout in the crow's nest of the *Resolution* sighted land to the northeast. All hands rushed to the rail, and as the ship surged northward through the blue swell of the Pacific, Captain Cook trained his spyglass on the emerging heights of a large island. Soon a second island appeared, directly ahead. Having observed both carefully, Cook made for his chart room and marked the ship's position with satisfaction. They had just discovered the Hawaiian Islands.

If the *Resolution* and the *Discovery* had veered northeast toward that initial landfall, they would have sailed right into what is now Pearl Harbor. But the direction of the wind made it difficult to approach Oahu, so Cook held straight north for Kauai. He was, of course, ignorant of the native names for these islands; in fact he was not yet certain whether there would be any natives. Inhabited or not, however, they certainly were an important discovery, for existing

69

A late eighteenth-century print shows the czarist capital of St. Petersburg, where Ledyard paused on his way to Siberia in 1787. Attempting to reach North America by way of Asia, he was eventually arrested by suspicious officials and deported.

charts showed the Pacific absolutely empty at this spot. Cook named them the Sandwich Islands, in honor of the Earl of Sandwich, First Lord of the Admiralty.

Now Ledyard and his companions were about to have a new experience: contact with a Polynesian civilization which had never before known Europeans or even dreamed of their existence.* As the ships approached Kauai, several canoes put out toward them, but stayed a respectful distance until the English had anchored and furled their sails. Then the canoes came closer, and the men lining the ships' rails could see that their occupants were bronzed young athletes not unlike those of Tahiti. Ledyard recorded that they "appeared inexpressibly surprized, though not intimidated: They shook their spears at us, rolled their eyes about, and made a variety of wild uncouth gesticulations." Considering that over two thousand miles of ocean had been covered since leaving Tahiti, the visitors were in turn surprised to find that these natives spoke a language closely resembling that of the South Pacific. Encouraged by an exchange of phrases, a few of them accepted the invitation to come aboard, and with many expressions of amazement gazed about at the products and creatures of another world:

They were exceeding wild; ran up to us and examined our hands and faces, then stripping up our shirtsleeves and opening the bosoms of our shirts to view such parts of our bodies as were covered by our cloaths. Then they enquired if we could eat, which we discovered [*i.e.*, revealed] by eating some biscuit. As soon as they observed this they ran to the side of the ship and called to those in the canoes, who hove on board several little pigs and some sweet potatoes. . . . They had no knowledge of iron or European articles, but the moment we discovered its obvious importance they were in raptures about it, and gave us any thing they possessed in exchange for it.

The crew gladly would have stayed at Kauai for the rest of the winter, but their resolute captain had other ideas. His attention was now focused on the search for the Northwest Passage, and he was determined to reach America early enough to take every advantage of spring and summer as the ships worked up closer to the Arctic. After two weeks of stocking their larder with provisions supplied by the Hawaiians in return for trinkets and nails, they set out again into the

---

* It was once thought that a Spanish navigator had touched at Hawaii in the sixteenth century, but this is now generally discredited.

Ledyard's Last Journeys

After the failure of his Siberian venture, Ledyard went to Africa to lead an expedition up the Niger. But in Cairo (shown above), a city which he described contemptuously as a "wretched hole and a nest of vagabonds," he fell ill and died.

huge expanse of the North Pacific. Conversation with the natives had indicated that there were several other islands in the Hawaiian group, just over the horizon beyond Oahu, to the east; but Cook decided to delay their investigation until later.

By this time the Captain had revealed to his men the main purpose of the expedition and the fact that King George had announced a prize of twenty thousand pounds to be divided among officers and crew if they succeeded in returning to Europe via the northwest. This made it somewhat easier to face a long siege of storms that beset them as they bore in toward the coast of what is now Oregon. Having caught a dim view of it through what Ledyard called "the ruggedest weather we had yet experienced," they tacked northward to the forty-ninth parallel, and then put in for a landing.

The *Resolution* and the *Discovery* sailed into Nootka Sound, or King George's Sound, as Cook patriotically named it, on the assumption that they were penetrating the mainland, and that this might be the fabled Passage. They were soon disillusioned on the latter point, but it remained for George Vancouver, coming back in 1792, to show that what they were probing was actually a large offshore island.

Ledyard notes that the explorers were uncertain whether this part of the world was populated "but we had scarcely entered the inlet before we saw that hardy, that intriped [*sic*], that glorious creature man approaching us from the shore." What he found very exciting was that the natives of Nootka seemed clearly to be "the same kind of people [*i.e.*, Indians] that inhabit the opposite side of the continent." Despite his service with the British Navy, Ledyard had never lost the sense of being an American; and now his heart was stirred with a strong feeling of national identity. "Though more than two thousand miles distant from the nearest part of New-England," he wrote, "I felt myself plainly affected. . . . It soothed a home-sick heart, and rendered me very tolerably happy." Doubtless it was at this moment in the voyage that he had his first vision of an adventure which was to lure him on for the rest of his life. Why not, some day, come back here and then tramp across the whole of North America to the colonies? It would be a feat worthy of an American Cook, resulting in well-won fame for himself and inestimable opportunities for his country.

71

The spring and summer of 1778 were spent in painstaking exploration of the coast from Nootka Sound to Alaska and the Aleutians, with time off to repair the ships, trade with the natives, and send the men ashore for exercise and berry-picking. Near the end of May they entered a deep inlet on the south shore of Alaska and sailed northeast, again "not without hopes," as Ledyard put it, "of the dear Passage, which was now the only theme." It proved to be only a deep estuary (now called Cook Inlet), and they turned back, disappointed. While there, they landed near the future site of Anchorage, and "took possession" in the name of George III (a vain gesture, since the Russians already had a well-established claim to the area). They also viewed with appropriate awe the mountain one day to be named McKinley, after an American President—the highest point, though they did not know it, on the North American continent.

In all of these events young John Ledyard was a fascinated participant; and now he was about to have a moment of personal glory. As they moved southwest, in order to circumnavigate the Alaska Peninsula, they began to meet signs of Western civilization: natives with iron tips on their spears, scattered articles of European clothing, and, finally, an Aleut who produced a note written in Russian. Nobody from Cook on down could make out a word of it, but since it was dated 1778 they had no doubt that they were intruding into a fur-trading area which Catherine the Great's entrepreneurs were currently working.* Cook was curious to see some Russians but felt impelled to push his exploration as far as possible before the end of summer. They therefore paused briefly at the island of Unalaska, and then made the final thrust up through Bering Strait into the Arctic Ocean. Here they soon encountered a formidable barrier of ice. No further progress being possible, they returned to Unalaska in early October, and now Cook decided to send someone in search of Russian traders. One man, he thought, could do better than a party. John Ledyard volunteered.

So it was that the young American was able to test his theory that he could make his way through uncharted wilderness alone and unarmed, depending for survival on his ability to get along with the natives of any country, especially if they were primitive. ("Like all uncivilized men," he had noted when observing the Nootka Indians, "they are hospitable.") He took with him no weapons, and only a little bread and a flask of rum by way of provisions. With a native who had claimed, by sign language, to know something of a white settlement, he made his way across the island, arriving by nightfall at a small Aleutian village where he was indeed hospitably received. Dinner—dried fish—was nothing to cheer about, but with the help of the rum Ledyard and the Aleuts managed to make a very sociable evening in the low, grass-thatched hut: "Ceremony was not invited to the feast, and nature presided over the entertainment until morning."

The next day Ledyard found a cove where a Russian sloop lay at anchor; nearby was a well-established trading station. Although verbal communication between him and the handful of Russians posted there was hopeless, he demonstrated his usual facility at making strangers like him. They plied him with such delicacies as boiled whale, dressed him in Russian clothes, and in the morning insisted that he take a steam bath. Three of them then accompanied him back to the *Resolution,* where he got a taste of acclaim from the whole ship's company for the successful completion of his mission.

It was now time to think of winter quarters, and Captain Cook headed back for the Sandwich Islands—with no premonition of the disaster that lay ahead. Coming in from the northeast, they discovered the island of Hawaii itself—Owhyhee, as Cook spelled it*—by far the largest of the group, and the most easterly. Although the men were desperate to get ashore, Cook cruised around the island for seven weeks while Master William Bligh made a careful survey. Finally, on January 17, 1779, they anchored in "Karakakooa" (Kealakekua) Bay, and Cook went in to the beach surrounded by a mass of canoes estimated by an officer, observing the scene from the rigging of the *Resolution,* at three thousand. Ledyard described the scene:

The crowds on shore were still more numerous. The beach, the surrounding rocks, the tops of houses, the branches of the trees and the adjacent hills were all covered, and the shouts of joy and admiration proceeding from the sonorous voices of the men confused with the shriller exclamations of the women dancing and clapping their hands, the oversetting of the canoes, cries of children, goods on float, and hogs that were brought to market squealing, formed one of the most tumultuous and most curious prospects that can be imagined. God of creation, these are thy doings, these are our brethren and our sisters, the works of thy hands. . . .

Cook was astonished not only by the number of Hawaiians out to greet him, but by their attitude. Somehow this seemed to go beyond what might have been expected even of people who had never met white men before: the moment he set foot upon the beach all the natives within view "fell prostrate with

CONTINUED ON PAGE 84

*See Robert L. Reynolds' "Seward's Wise Folly," in the December, 1960, AMERICAN HERITAGE.

*Since the Hawaiians had no written language, the first European attempts to spell their words were, to say the least, carefree.

AMERICA & RUSSIA, PART XI

The Communist party in America was so small, so faction-ridden, so isolated. How could it enlist so much popular support? How could illiberalism take in so many liberals?

THE GREAT DECEPTION

By MOSHE DECTER

Pure communism has been tried a few times in America by various Utopian communities, all of which eventually failed. Pure Marxism later attracted, relatively speaking, only a modest body of adherents. And the American Communist party, which was neither purely communist in the old sense nor true to the Marxist ideology, would seem—by the surface statistics, at least—to have been of no great importance either. At no time in its history, for example, did it have more than 80,000 members; it was an apparently ragged and hopeless cause, sometimes harassed but generally tolerated by the generosity of American law. That this was only the visible part of the iceberg many intelligent people long realized, but thousands, indeed millions, did not. How this "party," in effect an arm of Soviet absolutism, deluded so many liberal-minded people, how it penetrated so deeply and dangerously into the political and intellectual life of the United States, is the burden of the article which begins on the next page, and which concludes, on a most important note, our series on America and Russia.

In any discussion of this angry subject, the credentials and outlook of the author ought, perhaps, to be stated. Few writers not former Communists themselves are qualified to discuss the inner workings of the Communist movement. Moshe Decter is an exception. He was seventeen, he writes, when the Hitler-Stalin Pact focused his attention on the subject on which he has since made himself an expert. He was a combat infantryman in World War II, and has been a political writer and editor since. He has worked for the Voice of America, analyzing the party's line and activities, and in 1954 published *McCarthy and the Communists,* a book which, he says, "managed to be both anti-McCarthy and anti-Communist." He was managing editor, from 1958 to 1960, of the liberal, anti-Communist journal, *The New Leader,* and is at present writing another book on Communism and its effect upon the mass communications media in the United States.—THE EDITORS

Thus the famous muckraker after a visit to Russia in 1919. Thousands of American liberals agreed with him.

How could it have happened?

In March, 1937, eighty-eight writers, artists, teachers, and clergymen, many of them famous and successful, issued an "Open Letter to American Liberals," defending the "good name" of the Soviet government and denouncing Professor John Dewey's investigation of Joseph Stalin's charges against Leon Trotsky.

In April, 1938, a committee of five self-styled "liberals and progressives" circulated a statement—soon to be signed by 123 well-known artists, writers, actors, and musicians—expressing staunch support for Stalin's bloody purge trials.

In August, 1939, just nine days before the signing of the Hitler-Stalin Pact, some four hundred leading American intellectuals of the arts, sciences, and professions published a long "Open Letter" branding as fascists and reactionaries all those who expressed the "fantastic falsehood that the U.S.S.R. and totalitarian states are fundamentally alike" in their suppression of cultural freedom, civil liberties, and free trade-union activity. It is unnecessary, even if space were available, to print the names of all these signers, and to reopen old sores. The problem is not one of individuals, for we are dealing with a widespread phenomenon.

What made it possible—at the height of the most ferocious butchery ever perpetrated in Soviet Russia, in the face of the GPU terror in Spain and the daily political murders by Stalinists in France (all demonstrable and demonstrated at the time)—for scores, even hundreds of distinguished American literary, academic, artistic, and intellectual figures to come forward and deny these outrages, defend the purge trials, support the U.S.S.R. politically, and attack those who sought to bring out the facts? What was the state of mind of these people when they closed their eyes to Stalin's crimes? What made it possible for the miniscule American Communist party to score so devastating a triumph?

Here was a party that at any one time had no more than 80,000 members (although hundreds of thousands doubtless passed through its ranks over the years), and which for the first decade and a half of its existence was almost wholly isolated from the American working class—the very locomotive of history to whose destinies it had ideologically committed itself. Yet almost overnight this tiny, ineffectual sect transformed itself into an apparatus that could boast significant penetration of major U.S. government offices, complete or partial control of a score of powerful new industrial unions, the exploitation of the decent instincts and noble impulses of hundreds of thousands of upstanding citizens (the total membership of all the organizations affiliated with the most successful of all the fronts, the American League for Peace and Democracy, numbered about seven million at its height in 1939).

During the first fifteen years of its existence, from 1919 to 1934, the influence of the American Communist party was indeed insubstantial. Though it did manage to inject itself, in the mid-twenties, into a variety of trade-union conflicts, the results were nowhere near as impressive as the party had hoped. It gained control of the Furriers' Union; conducted a protracted strike of textile workers in Passaic, New Jersey; and captured Cloakmakers Local 22, the largest local of the International Ladies Garment Workers Union, leading it in a six-month strike. But instead of winning, the union had to settle for terms initially rejected by the Communists, who far from strengthening their hold ended by being driven from practically all the influential union offices. Instead of gaining control of the ILGWU, they virtually succeeded in wrecking it—a bitter experience that was enormously significant in American labor history, for it produced in the ILGWU a schooled, skillful, and sophisticated anticommunist leadership to guide other unions (if with only partial success) during their infighting with the Communists in the thirties and forties.

Factionalism and frenetic polemics had characterized the Communist movement from the start. Its roots lay in the Socialist party, which had itself passed through a number of important structural changes, ideological splits, and other vicissitudes since its foundation in 1890. For a number of years the Socialists had been led by old stalwarts like Eugene V. Debs, Victor Berger, and Morris Hillquit. Originally very much a native movement, with close ties to both midwestern radicalism and urban intellectual rebels, the Socialist party had come by 1919 to be dominated by foreign-born, particularly East European Jewish, immigrant groups, located in the great northeastern centers, chiefly New York. It included an unusually high proportion of well-educated, cultivated people who had already become deeply involved in various revolutionary and socialist organizations.

The overthrow of the Czar, the Bolshevik Revolution of 1917, and the feverish revolutionary activities in Germany, Hungary, and other European countries served as an extraordinary stimulus to the American Socialists. Even before the Revolution, there had arisen left-wing elements within the Socialist party that were critical of the old leadership's "class-collaborationist" policies, some of them centering around the Russian exiles living in New York, such as Leon Trotsky and Nikolai Bukharin. By April, 1919, the Third or Communist International (the "Comintern") had been created, revolutions had broken out in half a dozen European countries, and revolutionary regimes had been established in Munich and in Hungary. In America these seemingly millennial events, together with the personality and leadership of Lenin, swept the Socialist left-wingers—especially those in the party's various foreign-language subsidiaries or "federations"—off their feet. The following month the Socialist party—still under the old prewar, prerevolutionary leadership of Hillquit and Berger—called a referendum to elect party officials. Such an election had not been held since April, 1917, in part as a precautionary move to forestall government harassment, but already the leaders had become anxious about the incursion of the left-wingers—not so much because of doctrinal differences as because of a deep resentment of these unknown and untried young upstarts who threatened to take over the movement to which older men had devoted their lives. The May election confirmed their worst fears. The left wing captured twelve of the fifteen seats on the party's executive committee, and two of the newcomers—Kate O'Hare and John Reed—decisively defeated Hillquit and Berger for the vital positions of international representative and international secretary respectively.

Hillquit and Berger chose to ignore the referendum, claiming election frauds; they appointed an inspection commission and proceeded to expel, one after another, the left-wing foreign-language groups and various state organizations from the Socialist party. A convention was called to meet in Chicago in August, 1919, whereupon the left-wing forces called their own convention in New York in June, with the express purpose of organizing an attempt to capture the Chicago meeting. Factions erupted within factions, and an impatient minority within the left wing—giving up hope of taking over the Socialists—called for the creation of an American Communist party. A convention for this purpose was summoned to Chicago in September, a few days after the Socialist meeting, which itself broke apart into dissident groups. Thus was the American Communist party born, amid the wreckage of the American radical movement.

The Socialist party, which had begun the year with about 105,000 members, was decimated and left with something over 26,000. The Communist movement itself was split in three: the Communist party proper, dominated by the Russian Federation from the Socialists; the Communist Labor party, consisting of the English-speaking left wing of the Socialist party; and the Socialists' Michigan state organization, which soon renamed itself the Proletarian party of America. The left-wing movement had started the year with roughly 70,000 members, of whom some six or seven thousand had been English-speaking foreigners or native American members of the Socialist party. The splits at Chicago left the movement with only a fraction of its original strength.

For the following decade, schisms—and schisms within schisms—characterized the Communist movement. During the three years between 1919 and 1922, the major conflicts raged around the various Communist parties and sects, each maintaining that it represented ideological purity and the closest kinship with Moscow and the Comintern. By the beginning of 1923, the Comintern had succeeded, after repeated efforts, in inducing a kind of unity among the major warring parties, but these wars were only succeeded by bitter disputes and battles that raged for six years within the united Communist movement.

A certain amount of personal antagonism and strug-

SOVIET RUSSIA'S FIFTH BIRTHDAY

ALL ART YOUNG CARTOONS REPRINTED BY PERMISSION OF DR. ROBERT L. LESLIE

Jab from the Left

Nothing, perhaps, typified the attitude of the radical left so much as the whimsically acid pen of Art Young (1866–1943). A one-time Republican who heeded the call of the class struggle and became a Socialist, Young spoke for Communist and fellow traveler alike. Today, issues he espoused seem dated; but there was a time when they aroused thousands.

"All right, so far!"

gle between various sets of leaders is a normal feature of the life of every political party, but it is, with the Communist party, almost unavoidable. The first determinant of the fierce antagonisms which every Communist party harbors within its own ranks is constant failure to achieve its own aims. This was especially true during the twenties and thirties, when no Communist party outside the U.S.S.R. had the means of attaining power.

Leninist Communism believed in the effectiveness of small Communist parties, provided they were truly revolutionary. There seemed to be an assumption, never openly asserted, but always implicit in practical decisions, that the masses would surely follow the party, provided only that it was the right sort of Communist party. The inevitable result was that leaders and leading groups were made responsible for events which they were, in fact, quite unable to avoid.

The double Utopianism which believes that everything can be achieved in the nick of time, and that success or failure depends on the quality of the "vanguard," naturally claims scapegoats with periodic regularity. But in time it becomes increasingly difficult to find scapegoats. Every defeat and delusion naturally tends to drive one set of leaders outside the party, or at least outside the leadership, until every possible opposition is excluded. What then remains? Since nobody any longer dissents, and nobody therefore can be charged with any responsibility, there remains nothing but to invent scapegoats where there are none.

In this atmosphere it is not of primary importance whether the scapegoat is sentenced on personal or on political grounds. The antagonisms within Communist parties frequently defy any attempt at a political interpretation. In the Communist party there is almost invariably first the struggle, and sometimes a split, and the reasons come afterward. More than once, desperate attempts were made to formulate the content of this or that disagreement which had or was about to split a Communist party; both sides were unable to say what really divided them. The one thing that was possible to say was that party affairs had gone wrong. And as the very suggestion that basic elements of Communist policy itself might be unrealistic constituted the crime of treason, nothing remained but to find an explanation either in the individual wickedness or in minor tactical mistakes of certain leaders.

Therefore, the factional fights within a Communist party have always and invariably been more cruel and ruthless than similar fights in other, less Utopian movements. A man who, working within the party, is personally responsible for the revolution's failure to come is, in fact, worse than an open enemy; against him every weapon is admissible, even obligatory. He is a "traitor"; for, in the Communist mentality, every failure—not objective failure, but the failure of the reality to conform to the Utopia—supposes a traitor. It is naturally not certain in advance who the traitor is. First there is the betrayal, permanent and overt through the fact of failure itself; later it will be decided who has betrayed. This means that the apparent tactical reasons for a split are never quite so real as they appear from the outside.

The basic law of a Communist party is therefore to proceed through a series of "purges" of "traitors"; this, in the end, helped first Moscow, later Stalin, to establish absolute domination over the Comintern and its sections. But it was only partly due to Moscow or even to Stalin; it was implicit in the "ideology" of the movement. Lenin himself had started with the idea of

---

Art Young, continued

RIVALS FOR THE MONARCH'S FAVOR

"Where are we going, Mama?"
"Never you mind where we are going."

an organization of professional revolutionaries, with iron discipline, militance, rationality, dedication, absolute centralization, and monolithic unity of policy and action. He stood for a very narrow party, a party to consist only of professional revolutionaries, who would not be accepted into the party simply by their own will. They would be selected by the party from volunteers, and they would be directed in all their activities by the central committee.

Lenin saw this narrow inner party of professional revolutionaries with self-imposed restrictions as a guarantee against "opportunism." He argued that the ordinary worker, by the experience of his daily life, develops, not a full revolutionary class-consciousness, but only the "consciousness of the trade-unionist." Only those who have theoretically assimilated Marxism and devoted all their lives to the revolutionary fight are reliable. As Lenin saw it, the poison of opportunism had been allowed to grow unchecked within the Socialist parties of the West. There must therefore be, in the international socialist movement, ideological control from an orthodox center over the whole party, and it must be subjected to rigid discipline. This is the idea of the Communist International in a nutshell.

Virtually from its inception, the Communist party of the United States was a Leninist party in character, structure, aims, strategy, and tactics—with all that this implied: its acutely *Russian* nature; its early dependence upon and speedy and inexorable subservience to the Comintern; and its inevitable and total subjection to Stalin.

Following Lenin's death in 1924, Stalin had begun to consolidate his position as ruler of the Russian Communist party and consequently of the Comintern and all its sections, now eliminating this competitor, now the other. First he had used Zinoviev and Kamenev to undermine Trotsky. Then he collaborated with the moderates—Bukharin, Tomski, and Rykov—in destroying Zinoviev and Kamenev. At the Sixth Congress of the Comintern in 1928 he was already preparing to administer the *coup de grâce* to Bukharin, meanwhile using him to finish off the absent Trotsky by charging the latter with "left sectarianism," a disease to which Stalin himself evidently succumbed within a few short months. Having completely eliminated the Trotskyist forces, Stalin could next turn to the completely isolated Bukharin, destroying him in 1929 with charges of "right-wing deviationism"—namely, opposition to Stalin's extreme agricultural and industrial measures—and the new era of extremism was inaugurated in all Communist parties.

The beginning of this period coincided with the total Stalinization of the party in the United States as well. This was effected simply enough by an American counterpart of the Russian purge, when the plenary meeting of the executive committee of the Comintern expelled the leadership of the American party—Jay Lovestone, Benjamin Gitlow, Bertram D. Wolfe—and their followers for insubordination and for hewing to the Bukharin line. That same year, 1929, the party emerged with a new and fatefully symbolic name: the Communist party of the United States of America, Section of the Communist International.

How, then, could this tiny, isolated, ineffectual sect, completely controlled from Moscow, become the effective manipulator of the ideals and passions of large numbers of non-Communist Americans? The answers are to be found in a strange confluence of historical, political, and psychological factors that began to

CHILD LABOR EMPLOYER: "*You see, it keeps them out of mischief.*"

"*What's he been doin'?*"
"*Overthrowin' the guvment.*"

emerge clearly at the end of the 1920's. It was not the Communist party that changed its nature and so transformed the objective situation. It was the accidental historical conjunction of the right circumstances and the right intellectual climate among the American intelligentsia which the party, unchanged in nature and objectives, was able to adjust to and so exploit.

The circumstances: They began with the Great Depression; then the rise of aggressive Nazism abroad and native fascism (Father Coughlin, Huey Long, Fritz Kuhn) at home; the New Deal; the Spanish Civil War; the emergence of the Soviet Union as the ostensible champion of collective security. The intellectual climate can be summed up in one phrase—the cult of Russia.

By and large, the liberals and radicals of the 1920's were rebels rather than revolutionaries. Their rebellion had taken many forms—expatriation and exile (the world of *This Side of Paradise*); experimentation in life and art (the Greenwich Village period); disgruntlement and disillusion with the empty slogans and the slaughter of World War I (the era of *The Sun Also Rises* and *Manhattan Transfer*); nausea over the philistinism and crass materialism of the Harding regime (remember *Babbitt* and "Gamalielese"?). In the early years of the decade relatively few had become political radicals, though their number was slightly increased by the reaction to the Sacco-Vanzetti case.

Like any historical generalization, these more or less arbitrary categories obviously fail to do justice to the kaleidoscopic flux and variety of the period—to the fact, for instance, that these and similar rebellious impulses frequently enough merged with one another. (Witness that remarkable phenomenon, Max Eastman, who before, during, and after the war was at once rebel, radical, and revolutionist.) But it is safe to say that the intellectuals who put their mark on this era and gave it its tone were essentially apolitical—rebels without a cause or a home. As for the politicals—the older progressives who had come out of one or another offshoot of Populism and the Bull Moose movement, the newer post-Wilsonian liberals, and the tiny handful of organized radicals—they were rare, isolated, lonely, and ineffectual.

By the end of the twenties and the early thirties, most of the alienated intellectuals had returned from either literal or spiritual exile. They found a turbulent country in misery and ferment; and when they rebelled once more—this time against the injustices and horrors of the Great Depression—they at last did find a cause, allies, and a home.

It is from this point that what can be called the cult of Russia begins to take shape. Properly speaking, that cult—which first became a significant factor during the Depression and reached its height during the Popular Front and again during the wartime alliance with Russia—should be considered not as one but as three separate cults: the cults of science, of progress, and of power.

The Popular Front of the 1930's was paralleled by the triumph of Popular Science. Sigmund Freud and Albert Einstein were no longer, as they had been in the twenties, the monopoly of the professionals, the highbrow aesthetes, and the bohemians. They were now enthroned in the middlebrow Pantheon, embraced by the pundits of the genteel journals and the parvenu intellectual Chautauqua circuit that had replaced the collapsed tents of Billy Sunday and William Jennings Bryan. Freud and Einstein represented Science with a capital S. Into the temple of popularized Science now entered, with the same trailing whiff of incense, the last of this secular trinity, Karl Marx.

But whereas Freud represented the science of the intricate individual psyche, and Einstein the science of the remote cosmos, Marx was the discoverer and the prophet of the immediately relevant science of society. Marxism was the science that proposed to explain the past, provide answers for the present, and chart the course of the future. The whole dramatic panorama of History, it was alleged, unfolded in Marx's doctrine, which laid down the iron laws that guaranteed the ultimate, necessary triumph of socialism and then communism.

Intimately associated with the cult of science was a cult of progress, and progress was a shrine with many different worshipers: Why, when so many problems cried out for solution, could not liberals and progressives travel the road to it in company with their fellows to the left, the Socialists and Communists? And indeed the road map provided by the Soviet Union and the Communist movement seemed to represent historical progress—no less, they assured themselves, than did American institutions. It became possible, in fact easy, for liberals to say that while we have *political* democracy (however imperfect), the Soviet Union has *economic* democracy (however imperfect). So they came to believe that both systems were equally progressive, even though one was somehow more equally progressive than the other. The Soviet system, after all, represented "scientific socialism," and it was *in power* in the world's hugest country, where the working class had triumphed.

The liberal intellectual, as has more than once been noted, is both fascinated and repelled by power. Generally unable to sully himself in the dirty quest for it in politics, too uncertain and torn by inner doubts to wield power effectively, intellectuals have neverthe-

The formation of the American Communist party coincided with the Red Scare hysteria of 1919–20. Rollin Kirby's cartoon commented approvingly on the mass arrest and deportation of radical elements by the Justice Department.

WHOSE COUNTRY IS THIS, ANYHOW?

less often displayed a fatal weakness for successful strongmen and mighty power systems. Maxim Gorky, the great Russian radical novelist, was appalled and dismayed by Lenin's brutal seizure of power in 1917 and, later, by Stalin's rapacious destruction of his peers. Yet in the end his resistance crumbled into acquiescence and co-operation with both. George Bernard Shaw was another pre-eminent example of the liberal (indeed socialist) literary intellectual who admired strong men, shifting his admiration in time from Mussolini to Stalin.

There were many lesser counterparts of these men in the West in the thirties, and they had a name: fellow travelers. The curious historical irony is that the term was invented in the early years of the Bolshevik regime by Stalin's archenemy, Trotsky, as a rather contemptuous characterization of those literary and intellectual figures who, though they supported the Revolution, lacked the courage to go the full distance and join the Revolution's vanguard—the party.

What made the fellow travelers contemptible for Trotsky—and later even more so for Stalin, who understood them well and knew how to exploit their weakness—applied also to many American liberals. They suffered from a triple guilt. They felt guilty about the iniquities and injustices of capitalism, which they saw revealed in America from 1929 onward. They felt guilty about their own relative comfort, security, and safety in the presence of the exploitation of workers at home and the excesses of fascism abroad—they were, after all, not workers or victims of fascism, but writers, teachers, artists. And they felt guilty because they could not muster the total commitment and involvement characteristic of the organized radicals—the Communists being the most militant of all and therefore the most admirable.

True, theirs was a largely unwarranted guilt for sins they had not committed, evils they had not wrought, weaknesses which in part did them honor. But guiltless guilt is precisely the kind that is felt most keenly and lays one open most readily to cynical manipulation or cruel exploitation.

In the darkest days of the Depression, it was not uncommon for liberal intellectuals and artists to think of themselves, vaguely and in one degree or another, as Marxists, or as committed to the future of the working class, or to one or more socialist ideas and ideals. A striking illustration—in which Communists, fellow travelers, assorted radicals, unaffiliated dissenters, and disaffected liberals rubbed shoulders in a mishmash of abrasive revolutionary comradeship—was a manifesto issued by an ephemeral front called the League of Professional Groups for Foster and Ford, in support of the Communist presidential ticket of 1932 (William Z. Foster for President and James Ford for Vice President). The manifesto, entitled "Culture and the Crisis," declared in part.

We, too, the intellectual workers, are of the oppressed, and until we shake off the servile habit of that oppression, we shall build blindly and badly. . . . Practically everything that is orderly and sane and useful in America was made by two classes of Americans: our class, the class of brain workers, and the "lower classes," the muscle workers. Very well, we strike hands with our comrades. . . . We have aligned ourselves with the frankly revolutionary Communist party.

Just as the Depression increasingly inclined many men of sensibility and intelligence leftward, so the election of Franklin Roosevelt helped eradicate the isolation of the radicals and left-liberals. Hitherto, they had had small hope of access to governmental power. F.D.R.'s election changed all that. It signaled the intellectuals' gradual achievement of influence at the very time when the federal government had suddenly become the focus of national hope and promise. Obviously, the vast majority did not go to work for the government, though the great eastern universities did become recruiting grounds for many bright young idealists who followed their teachers to Washington or found an outlet there for their noble impulses.

Everybody at least knew somebody who was close to the White House, or was on the staff of some congressional committee investigating monopolies or munitions, or found a spot in the expanding bureaucracy of the Cabinet or the old-line departments or the newfangled alphabet-soup agencies (WPA, PWA, SEC, RFC, TVA). Artists, actors, writers began to fill the rosters of the federal arts projects, which in their turn became the objects of Communist attention.

Militancy was in the air. It was not long before an atmosphere was generated in Washington, where political power was centered, and in New York, where political ideas were molded and disseminated—an atmosphere that was hospitable and congenial to all sorts of radicalism. Leftward-leaning liberals could begin to feel that they were all part of the same spectrum as the most militant of radicals, the Communists—the difference being only a matter of degree.

Roosevelt's recognition of the Soviet Union in 1933 added a significant, subtle dimension to this upsurge. Many otherwise uninvolved people in this country had felt concerned about the western democracies' treatment of Bolshevik Russia, from the time of the Revolution onward. The U.S.S.R. was, after all, an experimental society (like New Deal U.S.A.), moving toward socialism. But almost immediately the capitalist democracies had indulged in military intervention. (Vague feelings of guilt about it are apparently still widespread, for Premier Khrushchev and the whole Communist propaganda apparatus never lose an opportunity, at home or abroad, to use it as a stick to beat us with. We have George F. Kennan to thank for a meticulous analysis of just how halfhearted, disorganized, and ineffectual that intervention actually was.)

Intervention was followed by nonrecognition, cessation or limitation of trade, suspicion, and isolation. (The other side of the coin—that this suspicion and isolation was largely the reaction to the open, explicit, and incessantly reiterated Bolshevik declaration of revolutionary war against the bourgeois world—was curiously but invariably ignored by America's liberals.)

The recognition of the Soviet Union by the United States at once removed the burden of guilt and enhanced the prestige not only of the U.S.S.R. itself, but of the domestic political movement associated with it. To be an American Communist, or a fellow traveler, or a sympathizer, or even a friendly critic, could become a matter of some pride (certainly not shame) in an atmosphere generated by a New Deal whose domestic policies—bold incursions on the evils of laissez-faire capitalism, and courageous support of the ex-

For a vast number of liberals who sympathized with the aims of the Communist party in the 30's, the Russo-German pact of 1939 was one betrayal too many. Here, in a cartoon entitled Another Lost Battalion, *J. N. Darling caricatured the agonizing dilemma that confronted fellow travelers.*

plosively burgeoning labor movement—accompanied increasing friendliness toward the Soviet Union.

For Moscow, recognition by the United States represented a significant diplomatic and political breakthrough, at the very time when the Kremlin and the Comintern were just beginning to think of drastically shifting their political line in the light of a new constellation of world forces. Not the Depression, nor the election of Roosevelt, nor the New Deal program, nor the recognition of the U.S.S.R. would alone have sufficed to forge the link between the left-liberals and the Communists. What gave a real lift to the Popular Front mentality of the middle and late thirties was the growing threat of fascism. Successful fascism affected everyone; a fight against it was a fight for survival.

In this battle, liberals and radicals alike could commit themselves to such simple things as anti-fascism, peace, and democracy. It was then that Moscow, having contributed so cynically and significantly to Hitler's rise, shifted gears. From 1929 to 1935, the policy of the Kremlin and its creature, the Comintern, was ultrarevolutionary. The theory was proclaimed that every member of the Socialist parties throughout the world and every trade union member was an active enemy of the proletariat. The Socialists were "social fascists." Democracy and fascism were declared to be identical. He who fought democracy also fought fascism.

This disastrous policy actually led the Communists of Germany, at Moscow's behest, to collaborate with the Nazis, not only in physical assaults on the Socialists, but in attempting to destroy the Weimar Republic itself. It clearly implied that the overthrow of democracy represented progress, that a Nazi regime was preferable to a democratic regime: it would itself be transformed shortly, by actual revolution, into a Communist one.

But with the complete triumph of the Nazis, the utter destruction of the German Communist party, the rise of clerical fascism in Austria in 1934, the nearly successful rightist coup in France in 1934, Moscow came to see both the threat to itself and the means by which it could turn the threat to its own advantage. A new chapter of Communist history was opened. With amazing speed, all the principles of "left extremism" were thrown overboard. Russia sought allies, joined the League of Nations, which it had hitherto vilified, and gained U.S. recognition. The Popular Front arrived officially with the Seventh Congress of the Comintern in 1935, and the new doctrine was soon to unfold in its manifold glory all over the democratic world. Defense of the Soviet Union and support of Soviet foreign policy became an openly admitted, paramount aim of world Communism.

Since fascism had come to power chiefly on the fear of Communism, Moscow was quickly able to establish itself as the main enemy of fascism, and so the chief friend of democracy. Thus the greatest Communist triumph of the period was Moscow's seizure of a monopoly of anti-fascism, its ability to organize the anti-fascist sympathies and impulses of large numbers of idealists who had hitherto been only partly—and in stages—prepared for such an alliance.

One issue, above all, dramatized and rendered virtually unassailable the Communist role of leadership in the anti-fascist struggle—the Spanish Civil War. Spain represented a triangular tragedy: the violent assault on a weak, ineffectual but democratic republic by Spanish fascists, aided and abetted by Italy and Germany; the prissy, inept, and shortsighted reaction of Britain and France (for whom the Spanish republic was no less expendable in 1936 than the Czechoslovak republic at Munich in 1938), in effect sanctioned by the neutralism of distant, aloof America; the emergence of Russia and the Spanish Communists as the supposedly glorious protagonists of Loyalist Spain.

Moscow's military aid was in reality both minimal in quantity and limited in duration. It was just enough to turn Spain into a Soviet satellite, but not enough to win the war. The Kremlin's policies in Spain were part of Stalin's intricate plan to achieve an understanding with Hitler. In Spain, as everywhere else, the party dropped its program of social revolution; at the same time, Soviet force was to be used there to show Hitler strength—but not so much as to frighten him into strengthening his Anti-Comintern Pact. In Moscow, meanwhile, the old revolutionists were being decimated in the purges, as another sign to Hitler that he had nothing to fear from Soviet Communism (though this, of course, was not the only reason for the purge). And all the while that Stalin was wooing the western democracies with his anti-fascism and his new social moderation, negotiations between Berlin and Moscow were going on behind the scenes.

Small as Moscow's aid to Spain was, it was still the only help given by an outside power. But an awful price was exacted; Spain paid dearly for it, in money and in blood. The republic's treasury of gold bullion, worth half a billion dollars, was spirited away to Moscow. The aid was the whiplash by which the Spanish Communists, theretofore the smallest and feeblest of the Spanish radical parties, bludgeoned and blackmailed their way, within less than a year after the outbreak of the war in July, 1936, into control of every major institution of Republican Spain—the trade-union movement, the youth movement, the Army (especially its political commissariats), the Foreign Office. Prostrate, bleeding Spain served Stalin, no less than Hitler and Mussolini, as a proving ground for his military forces and his political commissars. At the front and behind it, the party physically liquidated thousands of non-Communist Spanish and foreign radicals and intimidated thousands more into silence.

Little or none of this was reported in the international press at the time. There were even some prominent American journalists in Spain who deliberately suppressed what they knew "for the sake of the Loyalist cause," or in order not to embarrass Russia. And when some few non-Communist radical voices were raised to protest, the Communist propaganda machine unleashed a vicious campaign of abuse—labeling them as fascist agents. Much of the liberal press in this country meekly, gladly, took the cue.

Thus the biggest price of all was exacted in terms of liberal opinion, which exalted the Soviet Union and the Communist movement as the leading, if not the only, champion of Spanish democracy and of collective security against the fascists. The North American Committee to Aid Spanish Democracy was the main front behind which these sympathies were mobilized; the Soviet stranglehold on Spain gave it the sympathy and support of men of good will throughout the western world. Victims of this psychology, people who fulminated against the crimes of Hitler and Mussolini, chose silence in the face of Soviet butchery in Spain, swallowed the fantastic lies spun out by Stalin and Vishinsky against Old Bolsheviks Trotsky, Bukharin, Kamenev, Zinoviev, Radek, *et al.,* and heaped scorn on those American liberals and radicals who sought the truth.

In such an atmosphere, it was not difficult for the Communists to mobilize the emotions of liberal Americans on a great range of problems. The anti-fascist fight could be conducted on a wide array of issues—against brutality, horror, and ugliness abroad, and against injustice at home. It is impossible to overestimate the crucial importance of anti-fascist, anti-Nazi sentiment in building the barricades on the far-flung periphery of the Communist movement: manifestos, mass meetings, picket lines, petitions—everything from Negro rights to the Okies, from Spain to China.

The Communists were well equipped to distill and siphon off these emotions into a huge cauldron of subsidiary organizations which they either created or took over—popular fronts, united fronts, etc. They had behind them fifteen years of tough organizational experience—and the cult of Russia.

This did not mean that every sympathetic liberal or fellow traveler fully accepted Communist leadership without question on every issue. It was the very nature of the "symp," as the comrades cynically and contemptuously called him, to stay outside the party, to be hesitant or mildly critical about one or another facet of the "socialist state" and its policies. But the key factor was the "symp's" inability or refusal to recognize the Soviet Union as a totalitarian tyranny, in this respect no different from Nazi Germany. Given this refusal, the Popular Front psychology ranged free, and organized association, co-operation, and friendship with the Communists became acceptable and desirable. It was not until the fellow travelers were disabused of their illusions about the nature and objectives of the U.S.S.R. that they were able to discern that they had been had, that their anti-fascist and democratic emotions had been manipulated and exploited.

For most of them it was the Hitler-Stalin Pact that provided this novel illumination. But for many it did not last—for as soon as the Nazis attacked Russia in June, 1941 (and the war, in the Kremlin's lexicon, was transformed from an "imperialist" war into a "people's" war), many of the old fellow travelers and a whole new generation of innocents came into the fold. During the wartime alliance, the party pushed such superpatriotic moves as the signing of no-strike pledges, the opening of a second front, and the prosecution of the Trotskyists as subversive of the American democratic order. And they succeeded in popularizing a whole new set of front organizations, the Russian War Relief, the Council of Soviet-American Friendship, the Council of Arts, Sciences, and Professions, into which a new generation of dupes (and some from the older generation) was inveigled. In 1943, Stalin, as an empty gesture of friendship to President Roosevelt, dissolved the Comintern; people were encouraged to greet this as a convincing token of Stalin's desire for friendship with America and his retreat from the old-fashioned goals of Communist world dominion. The following year, Earl Browder, carried away by his doctrine that Communism is Twentieth Century Americanism and by Communist collaboration with the liberal wing of the Democratic party (and obviously not discouraged by his master in Moscow), secured the dissolution of the Communist party and its transformation into the "purely educational" Communist Political Association.

Browder's experiment in collaboration with the capitalists was short-lived, however. In April, 1945, Jacques Duclos, the leader of the French Communist party and an authoritative Kremlin spokesman, published an article sharply attacking the "revisionist" and "opportunistic" wartime line of the American Communists, presaging the expulsion of Earl Browder from the party and the initiation by the Soviets of the cold war. It was not until several years later that the impact of the new line was fully appreciated by the American people. Thus, as late as 1947 the Soviet Union and its

David Low's classic cartoon summed up the shock and revulsion of the world democracies at the signing of Stalin's pact with Hitler.

RENDEZVOUS (1939)

satellites were officially invited to join the Marshall Plan, and 1948 saw the last flicker of Communist political activity when it managed to corral Henry Wallace and a few other liberal "names" into the Progressive party campaign (the nationwide Progressive vote was just over one million—admittedly miniscule, but more than the Socialist party had ever received, and sufficient to lose New York State for Mr. Truman).

Many who were not in the least taken in by the "socialism" of Hitler's National Socialist party were wholly enamored of the "socialism" of the Union of Soviet Socialist Republics. Many who would have been appalled at doing business with Hitler in the thirties were all for doing business and making political deals with Stalin during and after the war. Many who denounced the book-burnings in Nazi Germany were entirely indifferent to the making of "unpersons" in the U.S.S.R. Many who denounced Hitler's maniacal aggressions against Czechoslovakia and Poland found every conceivable justification for Stalin's aggressions against the same countries in the name of "security."

When in 1946 Winston Churchill growled out his ominous warnings at Fulton, Missouri, that a fateful Iron Curtain was descending upon the middle of Europe, the chorus of his left-liberal detractors included a galaxy of innocents who clung to their ardent faith that the wartime alliance with Stalin presaged the postwar birth of One World, in a peace guaranteed by the United Nations. This willful blind faith precluded a straightforward look at the grim events in eastern Europe—when, with the aid of Soviet troops and secret police, local Communists used all the refined instruments of intimidation and violence perfected by Stalin to foist Communist regimes on one hundred million unwilling victims, and so created Two Worlds. It was not until February, 1948, with the shock of the Communist coup in Prague, that many American eyes began to open to the consistent objectives and means of Soviet imperialism. Exactly one decade after Munich—and prostrated, democratic Czechoslovakia once more symbolized the folly of trusting a tyrant.

Even so, as late as the spring of 1949, a year after the Communists took over Czechoslovakia, the apparatus of the Communist propaganda transmission belt was able to corral hundreds of sponsors and scores of participants for the Cultural and Scientific Conference for World Peace, at New York's Waldorf-Astoria Hotel.

The phenomenon of liberal fellow traveling has lent itself to varied interpretations, ranging all the way from those who see it as a willful conspiracy to undermine our institutions to those who regard it as an attempt to cope with realities of political life in an idealistic way. The tragic polarization which characterized American life in the late forties and early fifties was in no small measure the product of the burden of guilt and confusion borne by a left-liberal community that had been duped and compromised—and by its lack of the honest courage to seek for the roots of its past blunders. As a result, the task of such an open, intelligent, responsible inquiry was abdicated, and left to those who had frequently neither the capacity nor the will to conduct such an inquiry properly.

At a time when virtually the entire American people was legitimately aroused by the incursions of Stalin's agents in Europe and of Communist infiltration and espionage at home, an important part of the liberal community thus cut itself off and isolated itself from its proper roots in the larger community. For the basic sense of the American people on the Communist danger was sound, when the intellectuals' was not.

So was created a wide and tragic chasm—one that yet remains to be bridged by understanding the true nature of the more novel, more subtle, more dangerous issues of the new decade. This regrettable, unhappy sequence of events contains a lesson for all Americans, liberal and conservative alike, who wish to interpret intelligently their own past so as to avoid being condemned to repeat it, at even greater cost. Today Americans and free men everywhere face a profound challenge from those exuberant, buoyant, single-willed True Believers who preach to us that our grandchildren will live under Communism, and who act on that faith with cynicism, flexibility, and perseverance. If the history of the past quarter-century can at all serve us, it can guide us to understand that they mean not peace but a sword, that they really mean to "bury" us; to understand further that the only way to cope with such a faith is to oppose to it a truer faith, more deeply and more gladly held because held by free men.

During the coming year, the America & Russia series, together with certain other articles on the subject from earlier issues of AMERICAN HERITAGE, *will be published in book form by Simon & Schuster, New York.*

For further reading: An End to Innocence, *by Leslie Fiedler (Beacon Press, 1955);* Heresy, Yes—Conspiracy, No, *by Sidney Hook (John Day, 1953);* Part of Our Time, *by Murray Kempton (Simon and Schuster, 1955);* The Red Decade, *by Eugene Lyons (Bobbs Merrill, 1940);* Where We Came Out, *by Granville Hicks (Viking, 1954);* The Roots of American Communism, *by Theodore Draper (Viking, 1957).*

Captain Cook's American
CONTINUED FROM PAGE 72

their faces to the ground, and their arms extended forward." A great cry of "Lono" went up, and with elaborate ceremony Cook was escorted by the chiefs and priests to a grassy pavilion. Various rituals ensued, none of which the English understood very well, beyond grasping that for the Hawaiians something highly important was taking place.

The explanation, it developed later, was that Cook unwittingly was playing a role in Hawaiian mythology. In a former age, so the story went, a god-king named Lono had departed from the Islands with a promise to return in some distant future bringing with him omens of peace and plenty. It happened that Cook's first landing, at Kauai the year before, had occurred during the annual feast of Lono. Now it was feast time again, and during the year that had elapsed the idea had spread through the Islands that the English, with their great ships and miraculous equipment, were Lono's immortal band, and that James Cook was Lono himself.

In John Ledyard's opinion, the trouble that soon began between the Hawaiians and the British grew out of the natives' gradual discovery that they were dealing with creatures who were, after all, extremely human. One human proclivity that led to the lessening of awe was the sailors' persistent desire for the accommodating Hawaiian girls, many of whom swam out nightly to the two ships despite Cook's orders to the contrary. Those orders, moreover, had been prompted not by any concern for chastity—Cook knew his seamen too well for that—but by the Captain's realization that his crew was spreading venereal disease among natives who had never before known this affliction.

But nature would not be denied, and even at the shore encampment, where Ledyard held guard over the tents, the attempt to keep Hawaiians and Englishmen apart soon broke down. Since the nonfraternization orders initially had been looked upon as having the force of a religious tabu, the fact that they were now broken with impunity raised considerable doubt among many natives as to the visitors' supernatural standing.

To make matters worse, Hawaiian economic resources were being put to a severe strain by Cook's demand for more and more produce with which to stock the ships for another long stint at sea; it seemed that there was not enough pork, breadfruit, yams, and bananas on the whole island to fill the maws of the *Resolution* and the *Discovery*. On the other hand, the British supply of nails, beads, and other desirable hardware for trade was running low, while some natives were getting bold enough to want more substantial articles, and to steal them when they could not be bargained for. Cook punished acts of thievery rigorously; the Hawaiians were obliged to see some of their fellows lashed with the cat-o'-nine-tails and others, including chiefs, held as hostages until stolen goods were returned. "We shall soon see the consequences of such conduct," Ledyard noted ominously.

Still, there were pleasant days during the latter part of January, when Cook and the old Hawaiian king, Kireeaboo, exchanged formal visits and entertainments, becoming genuinely fond of each other. The weather was fine, and the men enjoyed themselves ashore. Native girls performed exceedingly voluptuous hula dances; the English responded with a cotillion, danced to flute and fiddle—the music of the violin producing among the natives, Ledyard reports, "the most immoderate laughter." His Dartmouth mettle stimulated by the beckoning peak of Mauna Loa, Ledyard went with three friends to climb to its snow-rimmed top. They never made it, having underestimated its height (13,680 feet) and the thickness of the tropical undergrowth on its slopes, but it was good sport.

Now events took their last, sinister turn. Wanting firewood for the ships' stoves, Cook had the bad judgment to requisition the fence surrounding the Hawaiian's *Morai,* or sacred burial ground. A party went ashore to tear it down, offering the priest two or three iron hatchets in compensation. The bargain was indignantly refused, but the priests took no action to prevent the destruction of the fence: Lono had spoken.

Or was it really Lono? That, apparently, was the question that was beginning to bother some of the Hawaiian leaders. About this time one of the English sailors died of natural causes, and instead of concealing his death Cook had him buried on the island with a good deal of ceremony, thinking to impress the natives. They were certainly impressed, but perhaps what struck them above all was the fact that their troublesome guests were not, obviously, immortal.

The British departed from Kealakekua Bay, in an atmosphere of strained cordiality, on February 5, 1779. All might have ended reasonably well had not a heavy storm sprung the *Resolution*'s foremast before they were a week away, so back they came to make repairs. The Hawaiians were not happy to see them. "When we entered the bay where before we had the shouts of thousands to welcome our arrival, we had the mortification not to see a single canoe," Ledyard wrote. Violence between sailors and natives broke out several times within twenty-four hours; and now systematic thefts occurred as if in further effort to discourage a longer stay. On the night of February 13 the *Discovery*'s cutter was stolen. Cook was furious, and decided to take action in person. His plan followed a pattern he had effectively used at other islands: he would lure King Kireeaboo aboard ship and hold him until the cutter was returned.

Early the next morning Cook took two boats ashore with a guard of ten marines, including Corporal John Ledyard, and went to Kireeaboo's dwelling. Ledyard noted that the settlement showed "every symptom of mischief"; no women or children were to be seen, and very few men. The old king came out to greet Cook amicably enough, and seemed willing to come aboard the *Resolution* for a visit. As they walked back to the beach, however, several hundred Hawaiians appeared as if from nowhere, most of them armed and wearing thick, woven mats hung over their chests like armor. Things looked ugly, and Cook ordered his marines to beat an orderly retreat to the waiting boats. He had given up any idea of taking the king with him.

But it was already too late. The crowd was excited, those in the rear pushing and agitating those in front; and at this point word swept through their ranks that one of their chiefs had been killed by gunfire from the boats waiting offshore. Another chief, standing near Cook, made a threatening gesture. To frighten the natives, the Captain, who was carrying a double-barreled musket, promptly fired a load of harmless small shot at the chief. Since this did no damage, the crowd's boldness rose with its anger: the chief rushed Cook, who then fired a ball from the second barrel and hit him in the groin. The sailors waiting in the boats and the retreating guard of marines now began to fire into the crowd, while the foremost Hawaiians leaped to attack the marines with clubs, spears, and daggers. Ledyard, who was in the thick of it, describes the next few seconds:

Cook, having at length reached the margin of the water, between the fire of the boats, waved with his hat to cease firing and come in; and while he was doing this, a chief from behind stabbed him with one of our iron daggers, just under the shoulder-blade, and passed quite through his body. Cook fell with his face in the water, and immediately expired.

Thus the greatest explorer of the eighteenth century died on the shore of his greatest discovery.

Everything after that was painful anticlimax. Ledyard and five other marines got to the boats and back to the ship; four were left dead beside Captain Cook. The *Resolution*'s guns fired some cannon balls into the crowd on the beach, to keep them out of the bay, and the skirmish was over. That night and the next, several natives sneaked out to the ship bringing various parts of Cook's body. They were charred; Ledyard was firmly of the opinion that the rest had been eaten in some unpleasant religious ritual. More misery followed: in going ashore for water, the sailors met stiff resistance and ended by burning a third of the Hawaiian village and killing scores of their former friends.

And so, under a pall of bitterness and gloom, the English left the islands they had so happily discovered, to make a halfhearted second attempt at the Northwest Passage before getting under way, late in 1779, for home. It had been a dismal year, and their spirits were only partially raised when they touched at Canton, and found that Chinese merchants were delighted to pay tremendous prices for furs which had been casually acquired from the natives of Nootka and Alaska for a handful of trinkets the year before.

John Ledyard's life, after his voyage with Captain Cook, was short but fantastic; and in a sense his remaining eight years were a projection of that voyage. For at Nootka Sound he had been gripped by an obsession. He would return to the Pacific Northwest on an expedition of his own—not merely to make a fortune in the fur trade, but to realize his dream of crossing the American continent alone. He would open to his astonished countrymen the unmapped plains and forests beyond the Mississippi, and the name of John Ledyard would be remembered whenever men spoke of the westward thrust of American destiny.

But he was still a British marine when he returned to England in the fall of 1780. He was obliged to stay there until his enlistment expired early in 1782, while the American Revolution dwindled toward its close. Refusing to fight against his countrymen, he was detained in barracks for two years. Then, sent out on a frigate that cruised American waters for several months, he finally managed to jump ship, and joyously surprised his mother by appearing suddenly at the inn she ran in Southold, on Long Island, New York.

Back home after nearly seven years, Ledyard hurriedly worked his notes on Captain Cook's last voyage into a publishable journal, sold it to a Hartford printer, and set about promoting his project. His plan was to get sufficient backing to outfit a good ship, sail around the Horn to Nootka Sound, barter for a load of furs from the Indians, and send it on to China for fabulous profits. Ledyard himself, meanwhile, would have begun his great trek across America to the back door of the new republic.

But Yankee businessmen were as yet hard to convince when it came to such exotic ventures; and Ledyard's eye, they thought, had a too-romantic gleam. Discouraged after a fruitless year of hard work, he went to France, where prospects looked brighter. John Paul Jones was there, loaded with prize money from the capture of British ships; he took a keen interest in the Nootka scheme, and tentatively offered himself as a partner. For the noncommercial side of Ledyard's project there was even more impressive support in Paris. Thomas Jefferson, the newly appointed American minister, found in Ledyard a kindred spirit. He too had dreamed of probing the great western wilderness that one day, he felt sure, would be peopled by Americans; and Ledyard's idea of exploring it alone caught his imagination. They spent many pleasant hours talking at Jefferson's dinner table in the fall of 1785; and when, after weeks of negotiating, John Paul Jones decided that the venture was too risky, Jefferson was almost as disappointed as Ledyard.

"My friend, my brother, my Father," Ledyard began a letter to Jefferson a few months later when he was in London for one last try to find a ship for the Pacific Northwest. It was a salutation expressive of the deep feeling he had developed for the older man, and there are indications that in generous measure the feeling was returned. The last try had fallen through like all the others, and now Ledyard was ready to adopt a startling remedy that Jefferson had proposed. If it was impossible to secure a ship, why not go by land? Jefferson had seen ample evidence of Ledyard's strength, courage, and self-reliance: he seemed a fit candidate to attempt "to circumambulate the globe," walking across Europe and Siberia to the Pacific, and perhaps crossing to America with Russian fur traders.

It was an idea just wild enough to appeal to Ledyard, who after three years of frustration was in a mood for drastic action. His finances, as always, were low, but his morale was still amazingly high. He drew heavily on his fund of friendship with Jefferson and the Marquis de Lafayette, whom he had also come to know well in Paris. "I am indeed a very plain man," he wrote Jefferson just before starting out in November, 1786, "but do not think that mountains or oceans shall oppose my passage to glory while I have such friends in remembrance."

He little guessed what he was in for. With almost no money and less luggage, he doggedly made his way up through Denmark, Sweden, Lapland, and Finland, and down to St. Petersburg; and from there—walking, hitchhiking, living largely on haphazard hospitality—all the way to Yakutsk, more than halfway across Siberia. "He says," Jefferson explained to a mutual friend after receiving a letter from Ledyard, "that having no money they kick him from place to place & thus he expects to be kicked round the globe." But Yakutsk turned out to be the end of his luck. There Russian officials, evidently suspicious of this strange American who already knew far too much about Russian fur trade in North America, began to put obstacles in his path, and after maddening delays he went back some 1,500 miles to Irkutsk to spend the winter of 1787. Suddenly, with an abruptness and lack of explanation that would have done credit to a Soviet commissar, one of Catherine the Great's provincial governors arrested him, and he was packed out of Russia by sledge-and-pony express at the killing rate of nearly a thou-

A drawing by an eyewitness, John Webber, depicts the wild melee in which Cook and a landing party of marines were overwhelmed by hostile Hawaiian natives. The explorer (right, holding a rifle) died when a dagger was plunged into his back.

sand miles a week, to be dumped unceremoniously across the Polish border less than a month later. It had taken him half a year to cover the same distance going the other way.

Destitute, broken in health, Ledyard stumbled back to London in the spring of 1788, his dream of American glory splintered on the rocks of imperial Russian hostility. But his American spirit was intact. Concealing his physical condition and his desperation, he undertook, only a few weeks later, a dangerous project in a quite different direction. The Association for Promoting the Discovery of the Interior Parts of Africa, a group of wealthy English gentlemen, desired to sponsor an expedition to trace the course of the mysterious Niger River and locate the fabled city of Timbuktu. Would Ledyard lead the expedition, and if so, how soon could he be ready to go? "Tomorrow morning," Ledyard replied.

Writing to a fellow American diplomat in 1789, Jefferson sadly noted: "My last accounts from Ledyard . . . were from Grand Cairo. He was just then plunging into the unknown regions of Africa, probably never to emerge again. If he returns, he has promised me to go to America to penetrate from Kentucky to the western side of the Continent. . . ."

Ledyard had sent his mentor a courageous but disillusioned report from Africa. "Sweet are the songs of Egypt on paper," he wrote. "Who is not ravished with gums, balms, dates, figs, pomegranates, cassia, and sycamores—without recollecting that amidst these are dust, eternal hot fainting winds, lice, bugs, mosquetoes, spiders, flies, pox, itch, leprosy, fevers and almost universal blindness?" He was disenchanted with the Nile: ". . . a mere mud puddle compared with the accounts we have of it. What eyes do travellers see with—are they fools or rogues?" He compares the Nile to "the river Connecticut" in size; and one cannot help feeling that he also compared, in his own mind, the fetid Egyptian banks to the cool April green of the New England woods which had cheered his youthful flight down the Connecticut from Dartmouth.

On November 15, 1788, Ledyard took up his pen again to write the last letter anyone was ever to receive from him. "I have been at Cairo three months," he told Jefferson,

and it is within a few days only that I have had any certainty of being able to succeed in the prosecution of my voyage. . . . I travel from here Southwest about three hundred leagues to a Black King. Then my present conductors leave me to my fate—beyond, I suppose, I go alone. . . . Do not forget me. . . . I shall not forget you. Indeed, it would be a consolation to think of you in my last moments. Be happy.

Apparently it was only a few days later that, beset with a hundred irritations in the attempt to get started on his quest, Ledyard fell sick, overdosed himself with an emetic, and died at the age of thirty-seven. But if he did think of Thomas Jefferson in his last moments, he must have seen in his mind's eye the far-flung American West, still awaiting its first explorer; and there may, too, have flashed before him a glimmering montage of those splendid sights in Alaska and Hawaii which he had been the first American ever to see.

E. M. Halliday teaches at North Carolina State College. A frequent contributor to AMERICAN HERITAGE, *he is the author of an account of the American invasion of North Russia in 1918,* The Ignorant Armies, *recently published by Harper & Brothers.*

For further reading: Passage to Glory: John Ledyard's America, *by Helen Augur (Doubleday, 1946);* Voyages of Discovery, *by Captain James Cook (Everyman's, 1906).*

The Parson and the Bluestocking

attend the levees that she was in the habit of holding in her rooms for the benefit of her students and their parents. She had, however, nothing against MacWhorter, and with the arrogance of a de Staël and without waiting for a formal introduction she sent him a note, indicating her willingness to receive him but pointedly excluding Forbes.

Delia's initial objections to Forbes remain mantled in mystery. Catharine Beecher, Delia's staunchest defender, admits that she cannot account for them. But it was enough that she did not like him and would not have him on the premises, although she had known him since childhood and had even been a guest of his family. The slight cankered him vilely. The flirtatious licentiate applied a certain balm by reading the note of invitation aloud to his neglected friend and making good fun of a maiden lady, old enough to know better, unabashedly scurrying after a rich young man. MacWhorter also wrote a most entertaining letter to his friend, the Reverend Alexander Clapp, parson of the Congregational Church at Brattleboro, Vermont, describing the whole amusing episode and, without precisely saying so, hinting that Miss Bacon's behavior had been unbecomingly forward.

He concealed this state of things from Delia, however, and having finally gained admittance to her levees, rather rapidly cemented the friendship, which under this treatment shortly flowered into a love which was "pure," "fervent," but to Delia's annoyance and her family's incredulous scorn, "fraternal."

Victorian courtships were things of sighs and glances, of half-uttered exclamations, blushes and pallors, pleasing confusions, and devoted and particular attentions, signs as cloudy as the symptoms of typhoid fever but as decided and contagious as the disease itself. This one was no exception and was moreover carried on at one time in the full glare of Harriet Beecher Stowe, whose affidavit makes it clear that MacWhorter pressed his suit as zestfully as any pouter pigeon. "The most open, direct, above-ground, positive and explicit piece of wooing that was ever performed under my own particular observation. . . . such as nothing but a positive engagement would justify any gentleman and Christian in pursuing."

To do her justice it appears that Delia had doubts as to the wisdom and propriety of this courtship. She found MacWhorter's attentions disconcerting. When she appeared at the boardinghouse breakfast table, he would leave his seat to join her and pledge her in his second cup of coffee. His eyes followed her wherever she went. Other ladies in the boardinghouse rallied her on her conquest. Like Mrs. Stowe, they had never seen such unmistakable signs of devotion. Clearly MacWhorter was incapable of giving his thoughts to anybody but Miss Bacon. Children noticed it, servants noticed it, and, with some distaste, the Bacon family was forced to notice it. Delia was flustered. She feared that MacWhorter, taking advantage of the difference in their ages, "had chosen to insult her with unmeaning expressions of regard."

Common sense had a premature triumph, and Delia shifted her quarters to her brother's house, where MacWhorter took the earliest opportunity of calling and was as assiduous as ever. Delia's little nephews were employed as messengers between the lovers. Delia's mother expressed dissatisfaction with the turn of events. She asked her daughter what she had in mind. The answer was not very reassuring.

"She assured me again and again that nothing would induce her to marry him and that she much desired and must have the opportunity of telling him so."

Delia had, in short, maneuvered herself into the position of being forced to sue for a proposal of marriage in order to refuse it. In her mother's presence she wrote to MacWhorter, who had gone to Saratoga, and sent the letter off. He replied at once, and Delia dutifully handed the letter to Mrs. Bacon.

"It contained a declaration of warm, eternal, undying affection," declared Mrs. Bacon. "I distinctly remember the expression: 'I have loved you purely, fervently.' He assured her . . . that his love for her was a love which no change of circumstances could alter and that even though she should hate him it would make no difference: that he should love her in life and in death and beyond it." But there was a further unfortunate allusion to loving her "as a brother." Mrs. Bacon had never heard of such a thing as fraternal love between grownups, believed it to be an impossibility of nature and repugnant besides. Delia was reduced to telling MacWhorter that she could not be a sister to him, and he countered: "Was not another relationship possible?" What other he did not say.

With her mother's views so painfully clear, and mindful that her brother was diverted from antislavery legislation, the colonization of Africa, the annexation of Nebraska, and the conversion of China by his now thoroughly disapproving view of his sister's case, Delia decided to try a change of air. She set out for Brattleboro, Vermont, and MacWhorter came tumbling after.

For ten weeks Delia and MacWhorter remained at

Brattleboro. During that time he danced constant attendance. His thoughts, his looks, the very slant of his shoulders, were all directed toward her. They walked together, talked almost exclusively to each other—in fact so absorbed were they in their liaison that the other guests in the hotel where they had lodgings made themselves scarce when Delia and MacWhorter took possession of the parlor, rather than intrude upon them. To all of this the people who ran the inn testified exuberantly.

One person who was not convinced was MacWhorter's friend, Alexander Clapp, the minister of Brattleboro. He and his giddy young wife refuted the whole notion of a love affair between the elderly Miss Bacon and the young minister as absurd. Mrs. Stowe, however, had arrived in Vermont with her sisters and was satisfied that what she saw must lead to marriage. She reported her findings to her sister Catharine, and shortly after doing so she encountered Robert Forbes. Rumors of the "engagement" had reached him, and he was seething like a kid in its mother's milk. His friend MacWhorter was a helpless pawn in a series of nefarious moves by Miss Bacon. She was a woman of talent; MacWhorter was a man of property; she was of an unsuitable age. She must be a schemer. She had written him a note without benefit of a prior introduction, had lain in wait for him at other people's houses where he had not thought to find her. Her immodest behavior justified MacWhorter in amusing himself at her expense to his heart's content.

Mrs. Stowe was bewildered and distressed. "It displeased me to hear that you had written a note prior to the introduction," she wrote Delia later.

It seems little enough now—a display of reciprocal interest on the part of a lady and a gentleman in the restrained atmosphere of a family hotel, a few letters containing lofty sentiments couched in the ornate language of the era. The whole ritual seems so stylized that it carries about as much conviction as the antics of the figures in a willowware plate. But to the people of the year 1846 the parson and the bluestocking were chief actors in a drama as compelling as a bullfight, and New Haven society wanted its moment of truth.

It did not come. Catharine Beecher asked Delia point-blank what her matrimonial prospects were. When questioned, Delia proved as unmanageable at thirty-six as she had been at eleven.

"What shall I say if people ask me if you are to marry him?" inquired Miss Beecher.

"Say what you please," was the reply.

"Shall it be called a Platonic flirtation?" pursued Miss Beecher.

"Say whatever you think best," evaded Delia. She had been jilted, and she knew it. MacWhorter had returned to New Haven, and Leonard Bacon had tackled him with an excited request for an explanation of the attentions paid to Delia.

"What attentions?" asked MacWhorter. He vehemently denied that he had courted Delia Bacon. He would not have his friends think him such a fool, he told Forbes. There had been no sentiment on his side, "not a thimbleful." He had lent himself to the affair only to help Delia save face. She had shown a preference for him. She had actually proposed to him. In the circumstances he had behaved exactly as he ought.

Alexander MacWhorter defies interpretation. There is really no explaining him. If Delia had proposed to him on one occasion, why did he not thank her for the offer and be off? And if, as he now told Roger Baldwin, the ex-governor of Connecticut, she proposed not once but five separate times, he must have been insatiable for punishment to have remained in Brattleboro for ten weeks, conspicuously devoting himself to her, while perfectly able to leave town. Baldwin, who had submitted to MacWhorter's disclosures with reluctance, thought the fellow a rare fool and said as much.

The gossip in New Haven had by now, thanks to the misprized Robert Forbes and the Clapps, reached scurrilous proportions. Delia was totally compromised. Either she had been caught in a serious breach of decorum, or she was the victim of a shameless intrigue at the hands of that "clerical Lothario," Alexander MacWhorter. The Bacon family began to buckle on the armor of righteousness, and Leonard Bacon raised his hatchet-head like a tomahawk for the scalp of the licentiate. The young man was guilty of slander, libel, and conduct unbecoming a clergyman and a gentleman and should therefore be declared unfit to preach.

It was not to be supposed that MacWhorter and his friends would accede to this solution to Delia's vexations. He announced that he could produce evidence that Delia had been the active party throughout the whole affair and that if the Bacon family did not refrain from its persecutions, he would be forced to defend himself by making Delia's correspondence public. Robert Forbes and his cousin, Jane Fitch, claimed to have seen it already. In that case, argued Leonard Bacon, an investigation was imperative. Either a man was fit to be a minister or he was not, and if MacWhorter was innocent of the conduct imputed to him by Delia and her friends he must prove it.

No, said MacWhorter and his partisans. The licentiate would prove nothing. Let the Bacons prove their case.

Delia at first had hoped to close the chapter in the classic manner with the burning of letters and the remission of gifts. When she failed to receive her letters

89

and learned that they had fallen into the hands of Forbes, Clapp, and such girls as the satirical Henrietta Blake and the despised Forbes' cousin, malicious little Jane Fitch, she rose to a falcon's fury that momentarily shook even MacWhorter's leaden poise. Her ultimatum to him announced that she had seen the whites of his eyes and was prepared to shoot.

You certainly cannot but be aware . . . that the representations which are generally made here with regard to my relations to you are wholly and basely untrue. . . . You know that my regard for you was one which such a devotion as yours could hardly fail to inspire in a heart not wholly insensible to kindness. Need I remind you of that devotion? . . . The whole vocabulary of poetic feeling has been exhausted to convey it to me; not in writing indeed for you have been quite careful not to commit yourself in this way. . . . You have read my letters to your friends. Did you read them *all*? Were there no suppressed passages? Did you tell them of the circumstances that originated them? Did you tell them of those professions of impassioned sentiment without which they would not have been written? Did you tell them that I had distinctly *declined* the honor to which I am represented as having aspired? . . . Representations, the most humiliating to me, the most degrading that were ever fastened on a woman of reputation are referred to you as their author. . . . You have made it necessary for me to make statements on this subject in my own defense. . . . I had once some influence here and weakened and wasted as it has been, such as it is I will use it to the utmost. You may read [this letter] to as many of your acquaintances as you please. I do not wish for any answer . . . All I ask of you is to *send me my letters*.

The beleaguered MacWhorter received this letter at the house of Nathaniel Taylor, where he was staying. When his reply to it was returned to him unopened he glimpsed an alarming threat to his career. The Bacons were implacable, and if Nathaniel Taylor should take their part impeachment was virtually certain. In desperation he threw himself on the mercy of Mrs. Taylor and her daughter, Mrs. Noah Porter. He must have had stupendous powers of persuasion. In spite of their long friendship with the Bacons, which included Delia, and notwithstanding their undisguised disapproval of MacWhorter's protracted sojourn in Brattleboro, his protestations of innocence won them over. They promised to warn him of any impending crisis, by crisis meaning the moment when the business should come to the attention of his friend and patron, Dr. Taylor.

The crisis came that afternoon in the interval between tea and dinner, and gallantly MacWhorter met it, shielded by the crinolines of the Taylor ladies.

Doctor Taylor heard MacWhorter out sympathetically. Having endorsed the young man in the community, he chose not to take sides but rather to make peace between the parties and hush things up. With this purpose Taylor called on Delia, bearing with him MacWhorter's peace terms. Quite simply they were as follows: if Delia would abstain from defending her "delicacy" and withdraw her accusations, MacWhorter would suppress his "evidence" against her. If not, he would be forced to vindicate his honor by bringing a charge of slander against her.

The Bacon family, as one man, indignantly rejected such a course. Taylor's olive branch might as well have been gunpowder thrown on the conflagration. The Bacons would not hold their tongues, would not bargain, and would have the case tried.

The hearing was convened in Jeremiah Day's house (he had just resigned the presidency of Yale in the hope of spending his last days in peace). Twenty-three exasperated divines met together to try one of their own in a case of ill-considered coquetry. The parish clergy, headed by Bacon, lined up for Delia; the university theologians, for Taylor and MacWhorter.

Ponderously the inquiry lumbered on its way while the Day parlor shivered under oratory bedizened with classical allusions and ominous references to the Old Testament. Henrietta Blake, from the perspective of Cornwall Bridge, whither she had discreetly decamped following the receipt of a severe letter from Doctor Bacon raking her for having let her eyes fall on Delia's letters, fairly glistened with moral indignation as the mails brought her almost daily accounts of the trial.

"Poor Mr. MacWhorter!" Miss Bacon had remarked, among other things, that "Hettie Blake is doing her prettiest to obtain Mr. MacWhorter," Henrietta wrote her sister, Mary. Then came, one supposes, a Dickensian toss of curls, an enchanting *moue*.

"Now I think it very likely that I was doing my prettiest to Mr. MacWhorter. I'm sure I hope I always do to everybody and if I wasn't doing it to him I was making an exception which I don't suppose I did."

Sarah Thacher, Hettie's cousin, added a postscript: "All that I have to say is !!!!!!! ??????? . . . What *is* Miss Bacon made of? If I were a medical student I should wait anxiously for her demise in order to procure a post mortem analyzation. As to Mr. MacWhorter, his evidence seems to come out strong enough but I am not prepared to swallow *whole* all *his* simple negations. What a disgusting concern . . . Do you seriously believe that anybody tells the truth nowadays?"

The committee ruled that in view of Leonard Bacon's demand for impeachment, the burden of proof lay with him. His faction resorted to comparing Taylor to John King, the London blackmailer of women, while the defense retaliated by hinting that Delia had tampered with the correspondence made available to the court. Further, a witness was heard from who testified to the happiness of also having received proposals of marriage from Delia. Benjamin Silliman, Sr., who had seen her letters, saved her from the imputation of forgery. In the matter of the second charge Delia was able to prove that the surprise witness had proposed to her some years earlier and had been rejected.

Delia trembled and wept when giving her testimony; MacWhorter maintained an ineffable calm. He did not attempt to deny what could not be denied. He merely stuck to his original story. He was not responsible for Delia's misconstruction of his intentions. His behavior was perfectly consonant with that appropriate to a minister of the gospel. The issue was clear enough. Justinian himself could not have tried either Delia or MacWhorter for going to stay at a resort in Vermont, although both were guilty of doing so.

Silhouette of Leonard Bacon by Auguste Edouart, 1841.

The decision when it came showed frenzied footwork. Eleven of the members found for Delia, twelve for MacWhorter. On the one hand it was agreed that the licentiate had been "in a greater or less degree imprudent in his conduct." "But," rumbled the clergymen, "by which we do not intend to imply that what the aforesaid licentiate has reported of the relative of the complainant is true." They further advised that a committee of three should be appointed "to give with Christian and paternal kindness such admonition to him as in their view the case may require."

MacWhorter's Pyrrhic victory was a rout for Delia. Nothing short of his impeachment could have saved her mangled fame. She felt herself ruined.

"God does not need my labor," she cried. "He appoints me to suffer." In her outrage and frustration she turned to the attack on William Shakespeare, a subject that she had discussed with MacWhorter in happier days. Her journey to England, made with the purpose of proving her thesis, ended in the church at Stratford on Avon, where the sexton found her, mad as the baker's daughter, shuddering at the sight of Shakespeare's unopened tomb. She was briefly confined in the asylum in the Forest of Arden until her family, with whom she had quarreled bitterly, brought her back to Connecticut. She died in the Hartford Retreat, lucid and reconciled to her friends, and asking for a last look at the picture of her father, who had grieved himself to death because he could not bring the kingdom of God to the wilderness in his generation.

Alexander MacWhorter continued to preach the gospel and to bother his friends with his theory of the infinite indivisibility of magnitude and to puzzle them with the Baconian heresy to which he remained (perhaps sentimentally) attached.

In 1852 Henrietta Blake gave rein to her delightful perversity of taste and married him, to her father's unconcealed dismay. After holding a teaching post for a year, MacWhorter returned with Henrietta for a visit to Eli Blake and further infuriated the old gentleman by staying for twenty years. Mr. Blake, as one of his granddaughters put it, "was too honest to pretend a cordiality he did not feel." He was never known during those twenty years to have addressed his son-in-law directly. MacWhorter's own faction had come to regret the committee's decision. Vindicated, he lived to cause the Divinity School perpetual embarrassment because of his pusillanimous mode of life and the crashing dullness of his occasional sermons.

Leonard Bacon wholeheartedly forgave Nathaniel Taylor, and Eli Blake reaped the reward of his extended silence when MacWhorter concluded his visit to 77 Elm Street with his mortal span in 1880. Henrietta was inconsolable. She dutifully kept house for her father, however, until his death. With that event, which was long in coming, she shook the dust of New Haven from her sandals and ended her days merrily in a *pensione* in Siena, in 1901.

The investigation which had blacked the newspapers and wagged the tongues in 1847 was so far forgotten that people growing up ten years after had never heard of it. Delia, alone of its chief performers, is memorable. Her love affair was a badly managed farce, her life work, *The Philosophy of the Plays of Shakspere Unfolded*, is a marvelously contrived gargoyle, a monument to misapplied scholarship; and yet she emerges with dignity, a pathetic, even an engaging spectacle, like Ophelia, wearing her rue with a difference.

Martha Bacon, a great-great-grandniece of Delia Bacon, is the author of a forthcoming novel, A Masque of Exile. *Alexander MacWhorter, she writes, was "predestined" to be an uncle of hers: "Owing to a marriage in the next generation, he became an uncle to me on my father's mother's side instead of the uncle he would have been had he married Delia like a gent. But it goes to show you can't escape a New England descendant any more than you can an ancestor."*

The Sunny Master of Sunnyside CONTINUED FROM PAGE 40

ler's rotund city council—each alderman had been chosen by weight—snoring over the affairs of state; the ancient Dutch burghers smoking their pipes on the benches of their whitewashed houses under shade of giant sycamores, surrounded by clucking hens and cackling geese and grunting hogs; the parties at which many-petticoated Dutch damsels sat with their swains around tables graced with immense apple pies, dishes of doughnuts, and a huge earthen dish filled with slices of fat pork which the guests dexterously harpooned with their forks. Perhaps the most amusing scene of all is that of the storming of Fort Goed Hope by the Wethersfield Yankees, who in the middle of a sultry day, while the defenders slept soundly after a huge dinner, "inhumanly seized Jacobus Van Curlet and his sturdy myrmidons by the nape of the neck, gallanted them to the gate of the fort," and dismissed each one with a hearty kick on the heavy seat of their enormous Dutch breeches.

Irving also displayed a talent for genre painting. Take, for instance, his sketch of the Van Tassel farm in "The Legend of Sleepy Hollow."

It was one of those spacious farm-houses, with high-ridged but lowly-sloping roofs, built in the style handed down from the first Dutch settlers; the low projecting eaves forming a piazza along the front, capable of being closed up in bad weather. Under this were hung flails, harness, various utensils of husbandry, and nets for fishing in the neighboring river. Benches were built along the side for summer use; and a great spinning-wheel at one end, and a churn at the other, showed the various uses to which this important porch might be devoted.

The old farmhouse is situated on the banks of the Hudson. Over it a great elm arches. Beside it runs a sparkling brook. And hard by is a vast barn and an abundantly populated farmyard. This is rural life as Americans of the day loved to see it. No wonder Irving's tales were popular.

Irving—who in the preface to *The Sketch Book* had patriotically lauded the beauties of American scenery; who had exclaimed, "No, never need an American look beyond his own country for the sublime and beautiful of natural scenery"; whose skill at landscape had so impressed Washington Allston in Rome—reproduced exactly in his prose the gentle yet grand tones of the best native American landscape painters. Rip Van Winkle might almost be Asher B. Durand or Thomas Cole as, "late in the afternoon," he throws himself down on a green knoll "that crowned the brow of a precipice":

From an opening between the trees he could overlook all the lower country for many a mile of rich woodland. He saw at a distance the lordly Hudson, far, far below him, moving on its silent but majestic course, with the reflection of a purple cloud, or the sail of a lagging bark, here and there sleeping on its glassy bosom, and at last losing itself in the blue highlands.

On the other side he looked down into a deep mountain glen, wild, lonely, and shagged, the bottom filled with fragments from the impending cliffs, and scarcely lighted by the reflected rays of the setting sun. For some time Rip lay musing on this scene; evening was gradually advancing; the mountains began to throw their long blue shadows over the valleys. . . .

Crag, river, glen, blue shadows, evening light, boat on the water—these are the very trademarks of the Hudson River school.

Irving's age liked a vigorous emotional appeal, and Irving himself had reason to be sentimental. The beautiful young woman to whom he had been engaged as a young man—Matilda Hoffman, the daughter of his law teacher—had died before they could be married. Though it is not true (as contemporary biographers liked to say) that this tragedy broke his heart and forever put marriage out of his mind—later, in Germany, he became much interested in a Miss Emily Foster, and in France had a slight flirtation with Mary Wollstonecraft Shelley, the poet's widow—his youthful disappointment did cast a cloud over his life.

But Irving was too sensible a person to wallow in sentimentality. He was also saved by his humor, most of which is basically satiric. On various levels, the situations of the *History of New York* make fun of the phlegmatic Dutch and the overactive Yankees, of city authorities during Irving's own time in New York, of the Puritan chroniclers who started every history with an account of the Creation and the Flood, of Jefferson and the policies of his Administration, and finally, of human nature in general. Book I of the *History*: "Containing Divers Ingenious Theories and Philosophic Speculations, Concerning the Creation and Population of the World, as Connected with the History of New York," is a take-off on the early colonial historians like Increase Mather and his son Cotton (this was the original purpose of the *History*). In describing how one of New York's Dutch elders puts a patented windmill on the battlements and hires a trumpeter to defend the city, Irving is poking fun at the inventor Jefferson and his policies of nonintervention and peace before the War of 1812. Similarly, in "Rip Van Winkle" there is political satire in the questions thrown at poor old Rip when he comes down from the mountain. Ichabod Crane is a caricature of the Yankee schoolmaster, with his superstitious fear of witches and his avid desire to get hold of the Van Tassel farm, sell it, load his goods and Katrina on a wagon, and move west. It is not unsatiric that the foolish pedant ends up, as we are told, a member of Congress!

Yet, though the humor is satiric, nowhere does any note of bitterness creep in. Irving has no enemies; he makes one like even the persons he satirizes. Dame Van Winkle may have a sharp tongue, but she is otherwise a good wife, and her shrewishness is justified by Rip's shiftlessness. Ichabod Crane is greedy and absurdly superstitious and conceited, but his very absurdity prevents him from doing any real harm. The several Dutch governors of old New York are stupid, inefficient, foolish, and incompetent, yet they live in a fairyland where no real evil can happen. True, Dutch government is supplanted by English, the comfortable old era must yield to the bustling new, but neither nostalgic Irving nor his reader resents the inevitable change.

What Irving's works had, indeed—and this was their greatest asset—was personality, the warm, genial personality of Irving himself. Rarely in literature have the writings been so much the man. When Henry Wadsworth Longfellow met Irving, he remarked that he saw the author he loved repeated in the flesh. In all of Irving's writing, his biographer Charles Dudley Warner comments, one quality is constant—the flavor of the author. The writings are delightful because Irving was delightful.

In his personal life, he was generous and always loyal, possessing what Warner called "a boundless capacity for good fellowship." Every ship on which he sailed became a home, every officer a friend. After his death, Emily Foster (by then Mrs. Fuller), the woman he had wanted to marry and with whose family he had spent many weeks in Dresden in 1822–23, wrote of him:

He was thoroughly a gentleman, not merely in external manners and look, but to the innermost fibres and core of his heart: sweet-tempered, gentle, fastidious, sensitive, and gifted with the warmest affections; the most delightful and invariably interesting companion; gay and full of humor, even in spite of occasional fits of melancholy....

He had, she said, "a gift of conversation that flowed like a full river in sunshine—bright, easy, and abundant."

Perhaps, however, what Irving's age best liked about him was his gentle and persistent optimism. When he chose the name Sunnyside for the cottage on the Hudson near Tarrytown that he turned into the home of his old age, he was expressing one of his basic views. Despite his recurrent invalidism and his many pressing financial and personal difficulties, he remained cheerful. He tried to be like his character "The Contented Man" in *The Crayon Miscellany*, who in the midst of calamity was always glad for what he had. "I endeavor," Irving wrote as he suffered from dirty inns and vile food on his first trip to Europe, "to be pleased with everything about me.... When I cannot get a dinner to suit my taste, I endeavor to get a taste to suit my dinner." In the preface to *Bracebridge Hall* he wrote that he always tried "to see the world in as pleasant a light as circumstances will permit."

I have always had an opinion that much good might be done by keeping mankind in good humor with one another. I may be wrong in my philosophy, but I shall continue to practise it until convinced of its fallacy. When I discover the world to be all that it has been represented by sneering cynics, and whining poets, I will turn to and abuse it also; in the meanwhile, worthy reader, I hope you will not think lightly of me, because I cannot believe this to be so very bad a world as it is represented.

But—since geniality is not necessarily genius, and good humor and charm are not necessarily profound—Irving may have been right in his own appraisal of his work. Perhaps it never was his to "attempt a lofty theme" or "to seek to look wise and learned." His writings, though they are full of warm understanding of human nature, may indeed to some critics seem only "light and trifling." But on the other hand, Irving's "flute accompaniment" was exactly the most valuable part he could have played in "the national concert" of his time. Had he attempted to be profound, he might have sacrificed those qualities which made his work so enjoyable; moreover, he might not have attained the tremendous popularity that enabled him to open a way in America for the great romantic movement that was to follow and to prove to the whole world that good writing could be produced by and about America. Thus, though he perhaps cannot (as he himself too modestly admitted in the prospectus for *The Sketch Book*) "aspire to those high honors which are the rewards of loftier intellects," he has assuredly attained what in the same work he said was "the dearest wish of his heart"—"a secure and cherished ... corner in the good opinions and kind feelings of his countrymen."

Curtis Dahl, of Norton, Massachusetts, teaches English at Wheaton College. He is the author of "Mr. Smith's American Acropolis," which appeared in the June, 1956, issue of AMERICAN HERITAGE.

For further reading: The Life of Washington Irving, *by Stanley T. Williams (Oxford University Press, 1935);* The World of Washington Irving, *by Van Wyck Brooks (Dutton, 1944).*

The gatefold illustration on pages 43–46, Peter Stuyvesant's Army Entering New Amsterdam, is from the collection of J. William Middendorf.

It was midsummer, and by the calendar of the Foreign Dogs of the West, the year 1859. Word came to the royal Chinese officials at Peking that an American barbarian chieftain, John E. Ward, was at the coast awaiting arrangements to proceed to the capital. He bore a letter from his Emperor, James Buchanan, addressed to the Divine Son of Heaven, and he was also ready to exchange ratified copies of the Treaty of Tientsin, signed the year before and since approved by his Senate. He desired that the agreement, respecting trade at various ports, be put into effect.

But a barbarian chieftain representing the Country of the Flowery Flag had never before been permitted in Peking, within whose confines was the walled and moated Forbidden City itself, site of the Dragon's Throne. Therefore, extreme care needed to be taken to impress the barbarian with his country's inferior status compared with that of the great Empire of China. Was not China the center of the world, the Middle Kingdom? And was not America just a sparsely settled, barbarian state far to the west? Ambitious, to be sure, but if it wished to draw near the center of civilization, its representative had to conduct himself with proper deference toward the Throne and in line with the prescribed rites.

Still, the royal officials reasoned, let the arrangements for Ward's journey go forward. The occasion could serve to demonstrate anew to the populace their country's exalted position compared with that of a vassal state. With this worthy object in view, the first thing to be considered was the mode of transporting Ward and his party 125 miles inland to Peking from their ship, the steamer-frigate *Powhatan*, anchored near Pehtang. It developed that during a stopover in Shanghai, the barbarian had on his own initiative picked up two sedan chairs, one green, the other blue, and had requested sixteen bearers so that he and another leader in his party could travel in style and comfort during the overland part of the trip. But was there not some way to prevail upon him to ride in the rough carts traditionally assigned to tribute-bearing envoys? This would serve to notify the people en route of his country's lowly status. If he refused, perhaps he would be permitted to ride in the chairs part of the way, but certainly not into Peking itself.

The barbarian's mode of transportation, however, was of far less importance than the form of the Ta-li, or Great Rite—the ceremony he would be required to perform at his audience with the Emperor. From time

This lithograph of the 1880's, from China's first illustrated Western-style newspaper, indicates how ancient the kowtow was. It shows royal officials making obeisance (at the steps) during the T'ang dynasty in 689 A.D.

"I kneel only to

For centuries the world's envoys kowtowed to China's proud rulers. Then along came a crusty American with a stubborn pride of his own

By HORACE KNOWLES

immemorial, of course, all who entered the Great Interior to behold the Dragon's Face were required to kowtow. The entire ceremony consisted of kneeling three times and knocking the forehead on the ground three times at each kneeling. Whether Ward might have reservations about kowtowing was unknown, but if so, perhaps the required number of prostrations could be reduced. This would be a matter for the most careful negotiation.

For his part, the U.S. Minister was anxious to get on with the business at hand. He had been sent out by the President to perform this specific mission, and he had come north from Shanghai at the invitation of two Chinese Imperial Commissioners charged with arranging for the exchange of the ratified treaties. The Chinese also had planned to exchange similar treaties with the British and French, but their envoys had insisted on bringing warships up the Pei-ho River in a show of force and had had to be repulsed by Chinese forts guarding the river mouth. Ward, on the other hand, was willing to come with a small, unarmed party of only twenty men. He was in a hurry, however; stormy seas were expected, and in any event the *Powhatan* could not remain off the coast indefinitely: its supply of fresh water for the boilers was limited and could not be replenished there.

When word finally came from Peking that the party could get under way, Ward was told that bearers for his sedan chairs weren't available and that, besides, representatives of countries coming to Peking had never ridden in chairs. Ward argued that practically the only emissaries who had been to Peking in recent years were from countries under Chinese sovereignty, while the United States was on equal footing. The Chinese replied that his country was in the same category as Russia, which now had a representative in Peking who always rode in a cart, never in a chair; the rule must apply to Ward too.

Ward didn't know, of course, that Peking authorities were willing to let him use the chairs as far as the gates of the city, and in his anxiety to get the business over with, he assented to the carts. It was a mistake. In an argument with people who practically invented the status symbol and to whom face meant everything, he had lost the first round.

The carts turned out to be high, unpainted, boxlike affairs with no springs or seats and only a couple of cushions to ease the jolts of the rough ride. A little yellow pennant floating over the vehicles identified the group for the curious throngs along the way as "Tribute bearers from the United States."

John E. Ward

95

Eight days on the dusty road and on junks towed up the river by Chinese laborers, sometimes wading in waist-deep water, brought the party to the Morning Sun Gate at Peking. Hundreds of thousands watched silently as the first American representatives ever to set foot in China's ancient capital moved through the streets to their assigned quarters, a nineteen-room, one-story house in a residential neighborhood.

Ward's first act was to request a staff from which to fly his country's flag. It was promised but never erected; word was passed to him that the Russians had none. He hung the flag on a wall in the main reception room.

Negotiations looking toward exchange of the treaties got under way three days later. Representing the Chinese were the two Imperial Commissioners, Kweiliang and Hwashana, and also a Shanghai judge named Sieh. Besides Ward the Americans included two legation secretaries, Ward's brother, W. Wallace Ward, and Dr. S. Wells Williams, who also was chief interpreter; and W. A. P. Martin, assistant interpreter. Dr. Williams, who had acted in a similar capacity on Commodore Perry's historic mission to Japan in 1853 and 1854, had been a missionary in China for many years and was later to become professor of Chinese languages and literature at Yale. He kept a detailed journal of Ward's negotiations. Martin also wrote about them. (Later he would spend some forty years in Peking as a missionary and adviser to the Chinese government.) Ward's reports to the State Department and Chinese documents reveal other details of the mission.

As diplomatic etiquette dictated, the American Minister opened the conversation with polite inquiries about the health of his hosts, then spent a few moments discussing recent British activities in China and his own trip from Pehtang. But as quickly as might be, he got to the point. He wished to conclude his business as soon as possible, he said, because of the expected rough weather and his ship's limited water supply.

"Before the treaty is exchanged," Kweiliang observed, "it will be necessary to have an audience with His Majesty, who desires to evince his friendliness . . . We must consult together beforehand upon the manner of presentation at court, and it will be proper for you to practice the ceremonies used at an audience before the day appointed."

Dr. Williams had warned Ward that the matter of the audience would be brought up, for Judge Sieh had mentioned it to him in a brief visit to the legation the day before. And the ceremony was well known, as was the fact that the Chinese required that it be rehearsed several days beforehand. Ward replied:

In reference to an audience with His Majesty, I think it is highly important that I see him, not only on account of the respect shown thereby to my country, but the manner of my reception will do much to exhibit to the world the policy of the Chinese Government and enable the world to judge whether the proceedings of the English are right or not. [This was a reference to the British attempt to bring warships up the river.] I wish, too, to honor the Emperor and show him the same respect that I show to the President, which I have been instructed to do. In approaching him, therefore, I will observe such ceremonies and forms of obeisance as he may prescribe, except that I will not kneel or knock my head on the ground before him, for those attitudes

Ward and his party made their eight-day journey from the coast to Peking in mule-drawn carts (above) and, beyond Tientsin, in junks towed up the Pei-ho River by coolie "trackers." The springless carts, according

are confined with us to religion and are not used in coming before the President or before the ruler of any other country. In other respects I will accord with Chinese etiquette.

The issue thus joined had been a historic bone of contention between East and West almost since the dawn of civilization. The free and democratic citizens of ancient Athens once condemned to death one of their number, Timagoras, for disgracing the city by kowtowing before the King of Persia.

The West's dispute with China dated from the eighth century A.D. The first Arabian envoys to Peking almost lost their heads for protesting the ceremony; they got off with a severe reprimand after agreeing to perform it. The Caliph of Baghdad, Harun al-Raschid, hero of the *Arabian Nights*, also sent emissaries who at first objected but ended up complying. In 1656 members of a Dutch mission submitted to the requirement, and in 1720 a Russian named Ismailoff followed suit. So did a Portuguese envoy, Metello, seven years later.

The first British emissary to China, the Earl of Macartney, was ready with a novel counterproposal when he arrived in Peking in 1793. He had brought along a picture of King George III all dressed in his ceremonial robes, and the Earl agreed to kowtow to the Chinese ruler provided an official of equal rank kowtowed before the likeness of the British monarch. The Chinese ignored the proposal and got the Britisher's agreement to go down on one knee. They waived the head knocking. After the audience took place, the Chinese announced he had performed the complete kowtow, and the Russians in Peking, who had access to inside information at the court, confirmed the report. It raised a storm in England.

Another British mission headed by Lord Amherst (nephew of the hero of the French and Indian War) arrived in Peking in 1816. He also offered to go down on one knee and, in addition, to make nine "profound" bows in lieu of the nine head knockings. He and the Chinese argued for nearly a month, but his offer was finally rejected and Amherst left the city without completing his mission.

For their part, the Chinese saw their request for a sign of obeisance as a perfectly natural thing. Had not Heaven delegated all power over men to one person, and from the beginning of time had not that person been the Emperor of China? Were not the Chinese the custodians of civilization, possessing a superior way of life to which all men aspired? And were not all foreigners treacherous barbarians who harbored secret, covetous desires toward the Middle Kingdom and who had to be kept in their place?

Besides, the kowtow was simply compliance with the rigid body of ritual law which governed the social relationships between all people, from the lowest peasant to the Emperor, who himself performed the kowtow many times when he made sacrifices to Heaven or worshipped the Goddess of the Silkworms. Did this American barbarian now in Peking consider himself equal to the Son of Heaven?

The question probably never entered the mind of John Elliott Ward. He was, however, no less proud than the titled nobility representing other Western countries who had preceded him to Peking in years past. A native of Georgia, descended from the Scottish Highlanders who settled in the state in Oglethorpe's

Harper's Weekly, DEC. 10, 1859

to the Harper's Weekly correspondent who accompanied the party and drew these sketches, left the Americans "with very sore bones," but the junks were comfortable and the food, though exotic, was delicious.

time, Ward had been a reform mayor of Savannah and later president of the Democratic National Convention which nominated Buchanan for President.

The Chinese negotiators who heard his stand on the presentation ceremony probably were not too surprised; they knew the West's centuries-old attitude toward it, and they were prepared to negotiate. Commissioner Hwashana, described by Dr. Williams as a man of few words but those very much to the point, replied to Ward's objections: "Our rulers are equal, and so are we as their Ministers. Now, as we kneel before the Throne, if you do not, we become unequal, for you are raised above us."

"Not exactly so," Ward replied. "I represent a ruler equal in all respects to His Majesty the Emperor, and when I come before [the Emperor], I can do nothing which my ruler would not himself do. You are the officers and subjects of the Emperor and must obey his orders if you serve him . . . I cannot degrade my country by taking such a posture."

"I admit," said Hwashana, "that you are not the subject of His Majesty, but you are a Minister which is less than the Throne. If I were accredited at Washington I would unhesitatingly comply with all that should be required of me at an audience."

Ward acknowledged that he was inferior to the Throne. But he asked Hwashana and his colleagues whether, if they were in Washington, they would willingly do anything that would degrade China or its sovereign, or do anything that would violate the teachings of conscience. "Would you yourselves render religious worship to the President?"

Kweiliang took up the argument. "If I were in the United States I would offer incense before the President if required to do so, or sacrifice; and on the same principle you ought to conform to the usages at our Court. The envoys from Burma, Ryukyu, Korea, Annam, Siam and other tributary states kneel thrice and knock the head nine times, but they are inferior; your nation is equal and you need kneel only once and knock the head thrice."

Ward told him he'd just as soon kneel a hundred times as once. But he emphasized that his refusal to do so did not indicate any lack of respect for the Emperor, and he reminded the negotiators that the true test of respect lay in whether the homage was voluntary or compulsory. The Chinese argued that in Britain men knelt when they came before Queen Victoria to be knighted. Ward admitted that in some European courts ministers and subjects knelt before their own rulers, but when sent as their representatives to other countries, they never did and it was not required.

At this point, Dr. Williams' journal reveals, Hwash-

Entering Peking through the Morning Sun Gate, the Americans proceeded along a wide street thronged with curious Chinese,

ana asked Ward just what kind of ceremony he was willing to perform. The same thing he would do before a European sovereign, Ward answered: he would stand during the audience, covered or uncovered as the Emperor desired, though the latter indicated more respect; would bow as low as His Majesty required; would not sit unless asked to, and would never turn his face from the Emperor. But he stressed again that he could not observe rites reserved for religion.

"I kneel only to God and woman," he said firmly.

About this bowing, the Chinese wanted to know: just how low did he intend to go? Ward stood up. He bowed. It was a very low bow. But Judge Sieh spoke up: "If we don't prostrate ourselves before the Emperor we treat him disrespectfully; it is that or nothing in our view."

Kweiliang, however, softpedaled this view and sug-

turned up an alley, and came at last to the large house assigned to them: the former residence of a Mandarin who had lost his head.

gested that the negotiations be continued another day in the hopes that a compromise could be worked out. The Americans were quick to second the motion. The day was blistering hot, and the parley had lasted eight solid hours, the Americans sweltering in wool suits, the Chinese comparatively cool in their loose-fitting silk robes.

The discussion of the Great Rite was resumed two days later. Kweiliang began by stating that the Emperor would consider himself as having failed to show respect to the United States if he did not see its representative on his first visit to the capital. And he felt that since Ward was a plenipotentiary, he had the power to comply with what was simply a ceremony.

"I am not invested with powers sufficient to enable me to change the laws and usages of my country," Ward replied, "and can do nothing to degrade it."

At this point, he reminded the Chinese that he had come to Peking at their invitation, that when he had talked to them in Shanghai nothing had been said of having an audience with the Emperor, that the treaty didn't mention it and he had not asked for it. He called their attention to the fact that the Russian envoy then in Peking had not been presented at court, yet his treaty had been exchanged. Ward also said that he had trusted in the good faith of the Chinese, had brought no troops, and wished only to finish his business and return to his ship.

The Chinese were unwilling for things to reach an impasse. Kweiliang asked Ward to describe in writing the ceremony he was willing to perform, and the conversations were suspended for a few minutes while he and his translators prepared the paper. Dr. Williams' journal reports that Ward began by expressing his deep regret that the observances required of him at an audience with the Emperor were such that he could not comply with them, for he could not kneel or kowtow. But if His Majesty granted him an audience without requiring these formalities, the United States would regard it as an evidence of friendship, and Ward himself would count it a most distinguished honor.

I would enter the presence of His Majesty, [Ward wrote] with head uncovered, and bowing low; I would stand and not sit; I would not speak unless addressed and would retire by walking backwards, never turning my back until out of his presence. No American Minister has ever kneeled or made the kowtow before any sovereign and would be repudiated by his government if he should do so; no American ever performs either before his own ruler. I am anxious to manifest the utmost respect for His Majesty in every form consistent with the obligations I owe to my own government.

The Chinese considered it. But they had a change to suggest. In place of the sentence beginning "I would enter the presence . . ." they wanted to substitute, "On coming into His Majesty's presence, I will bend the body and slightly crook the right knee still standing."

Ward consulted his interpreters. Dr. Williams said that the term used by the Chinese for "crook the right knee" was almost equivalent to kneeling, and later might be construed to mean that. The substitution was refused, and with that, the Commissioners brought the five-hour session to a close. "We cannot come to any agreement," they announced, "and we must report to His Majesty that the customs of the two countries are so unlike that no audience can take place."

They did not, however, make that report. Instead, they worked out a compromise they thought would be acceptable to the court, and two days later Judge

OVERLEAF: Negotiations between the Americans and the Chinese officials began on a sweltering August day in what Harper's described as "the city hall."

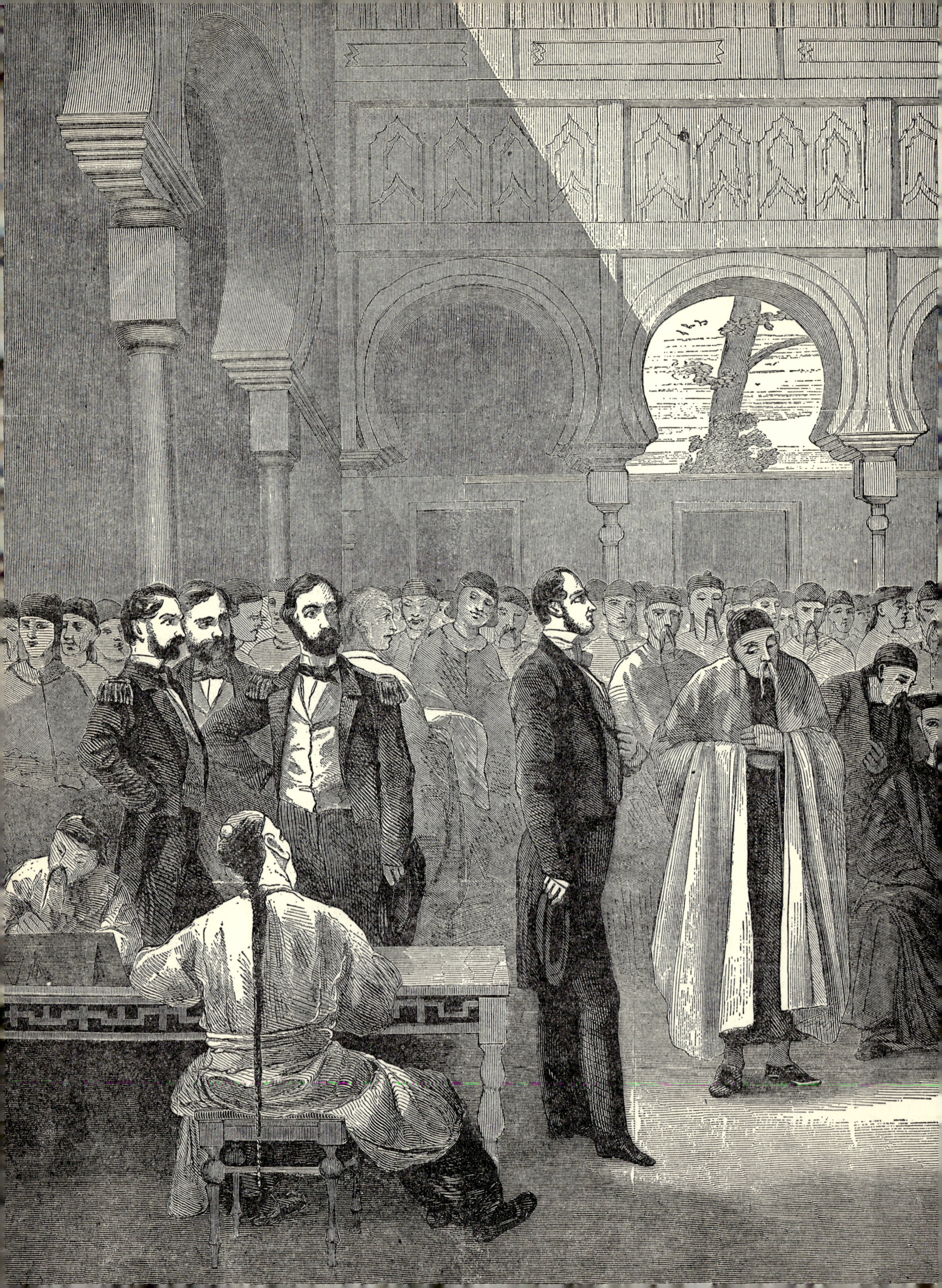

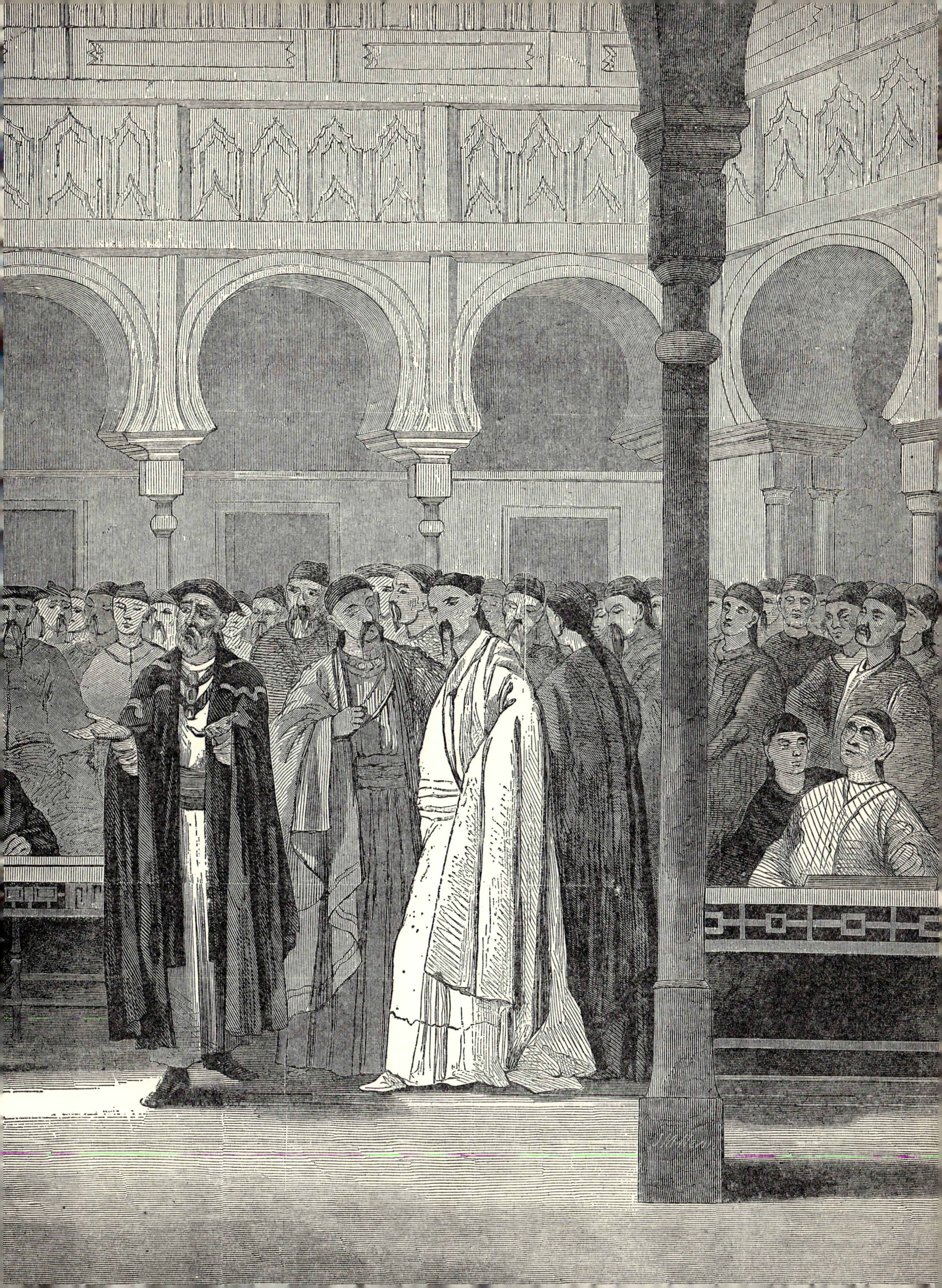

Sieh returned alone to present the plan to Ward. It went like this: Ward would enter the throne room bowing as low as he had shown them he would. Between him and the Emperor would stand a table covered by a long cloth that reached the floor. As he approached it carrying President Buchanan's letter, two court chamberlains would rush up to him on either side, seize him by the arms and plead, *"Pu kwe! pu kwe!"* ("Don't kneel! Don't kneel!") And they would raise him up, or pretend to do so. The Minister would then place the letter on the table. A court official would take it and, kneeling, place it in the hands of the Emperor.

Dr. Williams commented in his journal: "The cunning design of this table with an apron on it was to hide the republican knees of the Envoy from the Emperor, who might think he went to the ground if he liked."

Ward considered the proposal. Would it, he asked, be clearly understood that he had no intentions of going down on his knees in the first place?

Judge Sieh agreed to that understanding. "Nothing is required of you," he said slyly, "but when you see the Emperor you will be so overcome with awe that you will fall down of your own accord."

Members of Ward's staff became suspicious that the two chamberlains would throw him to the floor, but the Minister thought he could keep his feet, and he accepted the plan. The Judge beamed. Then it would be arranged. Except for a specific date, Ward could consider the audience all set.

But at 2 P.M. the next day the Judge was back, "dispirited and weary," Dr. Williams wrote. He and the two Commissioners had thought they could get their plan approved by the Board of Rites, which had the final say in such matters, but they had been outvoted. Still, the Emperor was concerned, Judge Sieh reported once more, lest President Buchanan feel insulted if his envoys weren't received. Therefore, would Ward not reconsider, meet them half way, and bow just barely low enough to touch one knee to the ground, at which time the chamberlains would instantly approach and raise him up?

Ward replied firmly that he would rather lose his head than kneel.

The Judge confessed he wasn't surprised at the refusal. But, he announced, to show the Emperor's magnanimity and his truly earnest desire to establish everlasting bonds of friendship with the United States, the Chinese now were ready to dispense completely with the requirement to kneel. He emphasized that never before had they condescended so far for a foreign envoy. All the American Minister had to do was bow low enough *to touch his fingers to the ground.*

So that settled that, the judge assumed. The audience would be arranged.

Now Ward had said he would bow as low as the Emperor wished. And the one he had performed for them was indeed a very low bow. But he'd said nothing about touching the ground.

Judge Sieh burst out, "It is only three inches more!"

Only three inches. Ward discussed it with his staff.

"Only three inches!" Judge Sieh cried. "What does that signify to make so much discussion!" And he advanced what he considered the clinching argument: Ward could tell the President anything he liked about the kind of ceremony he performed.

Yes, Ward said drily, that might do, for it was done all the time in China. But, he added, Americans observed a different code of conduct. And as for touching the ground with his fingers, though it was but three inches more, he would not do it.

When Judge Sieh walked out of that house "wearied and disappointed" at 4 P.M. on August 5, 1859, eleven hundred years of history came to a close. During that time the Chinese had brought to their knees the Arabs, the Dutch, the Russians, the Portuguese, and the British. But they had never met a free, independent American from the proud state of Georgia.

After John E. Ward had refused to kowtow or kneel or even to go those last three inches and touch his fingers to the ground, an audience with the Emperor was out of the question. But the Chinese never again made such a demand of a Western envoy. The next time the question came up, in 1873, the Ministers of the United States, Britain, France, Russia, and the Netherlands came before the Emperor bowing low once on entering the throne room and then three times before retiring backwards.

As for President Buchanan's letter, Ward delivered it to Kweiliang in a simple ceremony the day before leaving Peking August 11. He exchanged the treaty with a minor official at the port of Pehtang just before boarding the *Powhatan*. The fierce independence he had demonstrated at Peking was deeply ingrained in his character: when he got back to the United States he bitterly denounced his native state's secession from the Union and refused to participate in the Civil War. After it was over he moved to New York City, where he practiced law until 1902, only returning home—in the fall of that year—to die.

Horace Knowles, a public relations man, is the editor of Gentlemen, Scholars, and Scoundrels, *an anthology taken from more than a century of* Harper's Magazine.

For further reading: Americans in Eastern Asia, *by Tyler Dennett (Macmillan, 1922);* China's Management of the American Barbarians, *by Earl Swisher (Yale University, 1953).*

The Water War

CONTINUED FROM PAGE 35

Valley in quest of new sources. In the lower valley, where the city already owned most of the water rights, he sank new wells to tap the underground basin. And in the upper valley, which was still green with growing crops, his agents tried to buy water rights from the farmers in order to send a bigger flow into the aqueduct.

They found the valley organized against them. Leading the settlers were two brothers, Wilfred and Mark Watterson, whose five banks dominated the economic life of eastern California. Mark, the younger, was a good-natured mixer, inclined to follow the lead of his older brother. Wilfred, though more dignified and aloof, was nevertheless extremely well-liked; when meeting with a group of men he had the ability, as one observer put it, to "talk 'em out of their hind legs."

To prevent the city from getting further water rights in Owens Valley, the Wattersons conceived the idea of tying all the irrigation canals together in one large Owens Valley Irrigation District. With their customary persuasiveness they had put their plan over in an election late in 1922. But before the water rights had actually been turned over to the new district, the city made its move. Overnight two agents moved through the farmhouses along the McNally ditch, one of the oldest and largest irrigation canals on the river, offering premium prices for water rights. By next morning they had taken more than a million dollars' worth of options. When this news flew through Bishop, the people fairly exploded with rage. The city thought it had smashed the irrigation district? Very well, they would see that no water secured in the McNally deal would ever reach the aqueduct.

Soon every farm canal above the city's intake was gulping all the water it could carry, and overflowing onto marginal cropland. Below the last valley canal the bed of the river was dry as the desert. In the spring of 1923 Los Angeles was tapping its capital funds of water in the aqueduct reservoirs. In San Fernando Valley the crops were condemned to die. And in Owens Valley the city's predicament in paying for a million dollars' worth of water it could not deliver became an uproarious joke.

Mulholland had reckoned without the human factor. Embattled farmers at the source of water were threatening the very life of Los Angeles. In this frantic moment his water department made another error.

The last big ditch before the mouth of the aqueduct was the Owens River and Big Pine Canal, which was drinking in all the water not siphoned off by the canals upstream. At first the city's agents tried to buy water rights in the Big Pine ditch. But the Big Piners formed a "pool" and demanded rates roughly double those paid along the McNally ditch. The city agents thereupon resorted to what one called "primitive measures." The Big Pine intake was located at the point of a U-bend in the meandering river. One morning the Big Piners discovered city workmen with mules and scrapers cutting a ditch across the neck of the bend. If the river were diverted through such a ditch, the Big Pine Canal would be dry and the aqueduct would be gurgling with water. It was an astounding piece of deviltry for a municipality to engage in, but the municipality was powerfully thirsty.

Quickly the Big Piners rose to give battle. A posse of about twenty armed men—some on horseback, some in Model T's—poured across Owens River to serve what one of them called a "shotgun injunction." To the city workmen they gave stern notice: "We don't want any shootin', but we're not goin' to let you make that cut."

With that they threw the city's grading equipment into the river and settled down to guard the strategic bend. For two nights, relieving each other around the clock, the minutemen of Big Pine kept up their vigil. Finally, seeing that the city was not prepared to fight, they struck camp.

"Los Angeles, it's your move now," challenged the Big Pine newspaper. "We're ready for you."

Faced with this firm opposition, the city reopened negotiations for purchase—this time on Big Pine terms. Two months later the Big Pine farmers sold out for a total of $1,100,000—a price that made many a family financially independent.

Such rates now gave the water war a new turn. Seeing the color of the city's money, the other canal groups determined to sell out too. There were, to be sure, many families whose love of the land made them oppose sale at any price, but fearing they would be left to maintain a canal without the help of neighbors, they sold against their will. Still, from the moment of the McNally and Big Pine deals, the water war was chiefly a contest between valley farmers who wanted to force Los Angeles to buy them out at high prices, and city representatives who merely wanted to get the use of water rights they had already bought. To enforce their demands, the farmers of the upper valley continued to divert most of the city's water into their own canals.

By March of 1924 this strategy was working well. Los Angeles was getting so little water that Mulholland prohibited irrigation in San Fernando Valley "until we get a rainfall." Faced with destruction of their crops, the San Fernando farmers sent a delegation up to Owens Valley to buy a chunk of water. The Watterson brothers led a local delegation which escorted the San Fernandans along canals brimming full with clear Sierra water. Not one drop of it, said the hosts, was for sale. The entire upper valley, land and water, *was* for sale, however; it could be delivered in forty-eight hours—for $8,000,000. If the Angelenos needed the water so badly, they ought to be willing to pay what it would be worth in Los Angeles.

Back to the city went the San Fernando delegation. Within two months the city gave its answer. Suit was filed against the upper valley canals to recover the McNally and Big Pine water that Los Angeles had purchased. The Owens Valley people, fearing they could never defeat the city in court, prepared for violence.

On May 20, 1924, three boxes of dynamite were taken from the Watterson powder house at Bishop. A dynamiting job required no more than one or two experts. But some forty valley patriots assembled south of town for the excitement. In a caravan of cars the conspirators filed down the valley highway that evening while bystanders stood gaping. A few miles north of the town of Lone Pine they pulled off the road and began their work. Shortly after 1 A.M., the lower valley was awakened as if by an earthquake. Forty feet of concrete ditch was blasted away, but a great shower of rocks fell back into the hole and prevented most of the water from escaping. Quickly the dynamiters scattered over byroads to find their way back to Bishop while the valley came alive with the frantic activity of city aqueduct employees.

The preliminary skirmishing was over; the water contest had become a shooting war. Enraged at this attack on his aqueduct, Mulholland hurled a diatribe against Owens Valley ranchers that included such terms as "yellow" and "barking dogs." From the north came immediate warning that if he ever set foot in Bishop he would be lynched.

"They wouldn't have the nerve," roared the old fighter. "I'd just as soon walk the whole length of Owens Valley unarmed."

But the valley men had succeeded in rousing the city's interest in their plight. From the south came a parade of excited Angelenos—reporters, committees, engineers, and finally the Los Angeles water board. Accompanying its members was Mulholland, who made good his defiance of Owens Valley hotheads. At Bishop they were told by Wilfred Watterson that the only fair solution was to buy the whole district. Instead, when the commissioners returned to Los Angeles they drew up a plan to insure a sufficient water supply for the remaining valley farmers. They further promised, in compensation for loss of business from previous land purchases, to help build up the valley communities by highway improvements that would increase tourist trade.

A month later the valley gave its answer—in violence. On the morning of November 16, 1924, Mark Watterson led a little army of between sixty and a hundred men in an auto parade down the length of Owens Valley. They seized the aqueduct at the Alabama Gates, near Lone Pine, and turned the water out through an overflow spillway. Almost immediately the city's representative in the valley, Edward F. Leahey, arrived at the gates, in defiance of a warning to stay away. Leaving his car at the foot of the hill, he hiked up the slope to the wheelhouse. Through one of its windows a noose suddenly appeared and dangled before his eyes. Without blanching, he continued to the top. Six men, including Watterson, met him.

"Who's in charge here?" Leahey demanded.

"We're all in charge," returned Watterson.

"You can't contend we have no right to this water," shouted Leahey. "It's not hurting anybody going down the ditch."

"Don't you realize," Watterson snapped, "that whether people are damaged or think they are, the effect is the same?"

The strategy was plain enough. This was not an attempt to seize water, for the aqueduct was located downstream from the valley's center of resistance. It was a demonstration, through which the valley hoped at most to force the city to buy them out, and at least to publicize the affair throughout California. To the reporters who quickly gathered, the settlers gave their manifesto: "We are here to keep this spillway open. We will stay here until we are driven out or dragged out."

Against this threat Los Angeles first tried legal action. The local sheriff soon arrived on the scene and served seventy-five copies of a restraining order. But the men at the gates simply threw them into the rushing spillway. Then they picked up the sheriff and carried him in a sitting position back to his car.

The city next tried to get warrants for the arrest of the demonstrators. But the valley judge, sympathizing with the ranchers, declared himself disqualified to act. The men at the spillway were left to laugh at the law.

Exasperated, the Los Angeles water department sent a request for help to neighboring sheriffs in southern California. Their combined forces were then offered in support of the Owens Valley sheriff. But he was busy pleading with Governor F. W. Richardson to call out the National Guard—an idea which the Governor steadfastly resisted.

By this time the stand at the Alabama Gates had

become a grand picnic for the valley settlers. Up in Bishop practically every store was closed. On the flagpole in the center of town hung a large sign: "If I am not on the job, you can find me at the aqueduct." At the gates, ranchers and businessmen gathered about campfires in cheerful conversation while their wives brought hot meals from nearby homes. The congenial crowd had swelled to fifteen hundred, many of whom had brought stoves, tents, and beds. On the fourth day they had a barbecue, entertained the sheriff, and even invited the city's own aqueduct employees.

But later on their intensity of purpose returned. Gathered earnestly around the fires, the farm families passed along hymn books brought by the Baptist minister of Bishop. Soon the mighty strains of "Onward, Christian Soldiers" floated across the valley. For these stalwarts, Satan was a city, and they battled for the Lord.

That righteous refrain was not lost on the outside world. The story of California's little civil war was headlined across the nation and featured as far away as France and Sweden. Throughout the state, resentment against the upstart city of Los Angeles put sympathy on the side of the farmers. Even in Los Angeles sentiment was divided, though William Randolph Hearst's *Examiner* charged that the seizure was the "big card in a gigantic holdup scheme."

By no coincidence, Wilfred Watterson was in Los Angeles when the demonstration occurred. Meeting with his fellow bankers of the Clearing House Association, he addressed them for an hour, recommending the outright purchase of the Owens Valley Irrigation District. Here, of course, was the principal aim of the valley plan. Los Angeles might call it a "holdup," but the embattled farmers believed they were simply giving forceful emphasis to their plea to "buy us all or leave us alone." Since Los Angeles had not listened, they had done something to make it listen.

But for Wilfred Watterson the Los Angeles bankers had short words. Unless he got the gates closed, they are said to have told him, they would cut off his bank's credit. They agreed, however, to use their "best efforts with the business interests of this city to bring about an equitable settlement." Back to the valley went Watterson. Meeting with leaders of the spillway crowd, he asked them to disperse in response to the promise of the Los Angeles bankers. After holding the water supply of a great city in their hands for four days, they went back to their homes.

While the negotiations immediately following the gate seizure came to nothing, the valley people had made one point: they had convinced the Los Angeles water board that it could not afford to get its water from a hostile community. Up to Owens Valley went a top city representative to assess the situation. Returning, he went before the water commissioners and told them the bitter truth.

"The only way to settle things up there," he said, "is to buy out the rest of the valley."

"My God!" cried one of the members. "How much will that cost?"

"Five or six million dollars," was the cool answer.

Such a figure was far above any previous water investment. It meant both a tacit admission of past mistakes and a partial concession to the Watterson group. But early in 1925 the commissioners said they were ready to buy all land tributary to the Owens River.

Within a few days, Wilfred Watterson was in Los Angeles negotiating the sale of a large "pool" of property on the Bishop Creek ditch. By the end of March the city bought the entire length of the canal. It looked as though the valley people had brought the city to terms, and that the long war was over.

But one issue had never been cleared up. For years valley merchants had demanded "reparations" from the city to compensate for the loss of customers who had sold their homes and departed. Except for its offer to improve highways to attract tourists to the valley, Los Angeles coldly refused to accept any responsibility. The bitter question raged all the way to the state legislature at Sacramento, where the valley secured passage of a law to hold the city accountable. But Los Angeles officials then insisted that nothing could be done short of a test case in court. The valley people, with the farmer's inherent distrust of lawyers, refused to launch one.

Still another sore was reopened in the negotiations for city purchase of the last of the big ditches, the Owens River Canal. With only $41,000 separating the two sides in a $2,500,000 deal, the talks suddenly burst into loud recriminations. The Watterson brothers and one of the city men almost came to blows before they were separated. Almost immediately after the negotiations were broken off, city wells in the Bishop area

MRS. H. N. CLEMENT

If I am not on the JOB You can find me at the AQUEDUCT

Merchants in Bishop, center of valley resistance to the aqueduct, took part in the seizure of the Alabama Gates in November of 1924, leaving this sign at the town's flagpole.

were dynamited, and another "shot" was planted in the side of the aqueduct.

After a temporary truce, the war had erupted more furiously than before. For weeks valley people were gathering their forces for what one of them called "the last stand." On March 19, 1927, they opened their campaign with a full-page ad in leading newspapers of the state, describing the valley's struggle under the heading, "We Who Are About to Die." Four days later the city replied by announcing a deadline beyond which it would not buy Owens Valley land. City agent Leahey was horrified.

"If you do that," he warned, "they'll start dynamiting again."

Ten days after the deadline passed, a valley rancher bought a large amount of blasting gelatin at the Hercules Powder plant in Martinez, California. A final letter was sent to various Los Angeles officials and civic groups demanding action before the city's policy would "inflame real American citizens to violence." When no answer had been received in two weeks, the violence began. Ten men descended on No Name Siphon, one of the largest pipe sections on the aqueduct, and blew it up. While the culprits escaped northward, the whole flow of the conduit gushed into the desert. Rushing up from Los Angeles to repair the break, the furious Mulholland told reporters he could not comment "without using unprintable language."

Close upon this blow, the dynamiters placed two more shots against the aqueduct system. With his entire aqueduct threatened, Mulholland at last decided to fight back.

Northward into Owens Valley rattled a special Southern Pacific train loaded with a hundred armed men—veterans of World War I. Up and down the aqueduct they mounted their stations. When their arrival was greeted with another blast the following night, reinforcements came immediately. The lower valley along the line of the conduit was virtually under martial law. At night searchlights scanned the highway for suspicious movements. Autos were flagged down, and the guards inspected the interiors with flashlights.

But the valley had only begun to fight. Nearly sixty Winchesters were shipped to the Watterson hardware store in Bishop, where they were passed across the counter into willing hands. Fortunately a pitched battle never occurred. But under the very noses of the aqueduct guards the dynamiters continued to lay a shot in the ribs of the aqueduct whenever they chose. There was a total of fourteen dynamitings within two months; "shooting the duck" had become the leading outdoor sport of Owens Valley.

Reeling from these blows, the Los Angeles water department turned its attack on the leaders of the valley, the Watterson brothers. Early in August two of Mulholland's men entered the Sacramento office of the state corporation commissioner.

"We have reason to believe," one of them reported solemnly, "that corporate funds are being used for dynamiting the aqueduct."

That night, at the request of the corporation commissioner, a state banking investigator caught a train for Owens Valley. What he discovered at one of the Watterson banks in Bishop surprised even the Los Angeles officials. Wholesale juggling of books had left the bank and various other Watterson enterprises approximately $2,000,000 short. An incurable speculator, Wilfred Watterson had sunk fortunes in unsound industrial ventures, and to cover his losses had tapped personal funds entrusted to his care by lifelong friends and neighbors. To the city water people, this explained his ravenous appetite for Los Angeles money—explained, too, his refusal to take the valley's fight into a court of law. Convicted of embezzlement on November 11, 1927, both the Wattersons were sent to San Quentin prison. The bewildered valley people suddenly found themselves without leadership.

Los Angeles had won a greater victory than it had expected. Moving to make a final valley settlement, it bought the remaining Owens Valley Canal in 1929. The following year the Angelenos voted $12,000,000 in bonds to "clean up Owens Valley"; with this huge fund the city bought up practically all the town properties in Big Pine and Bishop. Though the purchases took place in the Depression, Los Angeles paid boom prices that had prevailed in 1923—the year that its invasion made its first impact on the valley.

To the Angelenos it was an expensive and even embarrassing program—constituting an admission of gross errors in Owens Valley. To the valley people who had spearheaded the fight against the city it could be considered a final victory; they had won a fatter settlement than those who had sold out in the beginning. But to most of the settlers, who wanted only to live out their lives on the land undisturbed, it was a tragic ending to a bitter feud. As they piled their belongings onto their cars and headed out of Owens Valley, they could echo Jeremiah's lament: "Our inheritance is turned to strangers." Wrote one of them, "It is not the loss of the home, or the garden . . . or the growing business which has been the test; it's the loss of the years, and the hope and the endeavor . . ." In the stunted remains of abandoned orchards, Angelenos may still see the swath their city cut in its inexorable drive for water—and bigness.

The exodus from Owens Valley was not lost upon

California's literati. Not since Longfellow's *Evangeline* had the dispossession of a people been the source of such pathos. Embattled critics charged that the aqueduct was conceived by the San Fernando land syndicate purely to reap swollen profits at public expense; that Los Angeles "forced the ranchers to sell to the city at condemnation prices and get out"; that it took water from the river forcibly without a legal right.

Even the Owens Valley people made no such claims. Fred Eaton and no other had conceived the Owens River project. In practically every case ranchers sold to the city because they were offered highly attractive prices. Los Angeles took extreme care to establish legal water rights from the beginning, and for several years it was prevented from using part of these rights because of forcible diversions by some of the ranchers.

But surely the Owens Valley episode offered Angelenos little cause for pride. At the beginning the city used questionable political methods to kill federal reclamation efforts in Owens Valley, gain rights of way, and hold water filings; it failed to build a reservoir at the head of the aqueduct that would have prevented the water crisis of the 1920's; and for several years it pursued a policy of buying only the water rights it needed, without accepting responsibility for the effect of this invasion on either the economic life or the morale of the Owens Valley community.

By the mid-1930's Los Angeles was moving to write the last chapter to its adventure by correcting an early mistake. Long Valley, the reservoir site, was purchased from Eaton and his associates, and the big dam was constructed in the gorge. Completed in 1941, it created Crowley Lake, which stores enough water from year to year to have supplied both city and valley back in the turbulent twenties. At the dedication ceremony one valley spokesman looked back over a generation of tumult and pronounced a weary finale:

"We cannot but regret that this enterprise was not constructed long ago; there would have been less of history to forget . . ."

Poetic justice would be served if it could be reported that the Long Valley Dam has made possible the rebirth of Owens Valley—that the farmers have returned to the land and are pushing back the sagebrush with orchards and green fields. It is tempting to declare that the one million dollars Fred Eaton had demanded for his reservoir site would have been cheap compared to the millions paid for Owens property.

But the relentless growth of Los Angeles has blasted the chances of any such conclusion. To provide more water for the mushrooming city, the aqueduct was extended farther north to Mono County; and although the total water supply is far more than even Eaton and Mulholland first visualized, the city's insatiable thirst has likewise grown. There is still insufficient water for a guaranteed supply to Owens Valley farms. What little agriculture is attempted depends upon short-term leases that permit the city to withhold the water at any time. Though early construction of the Long Valley reservoir might have averted a water war, Owens Valley would eventually have been sacrificed anyway.

Today the valley is sustained by the stock-grazing economy it knew before the farmers dug their canals— and by a growing tourist trade, for eastern California has become a year-round playground for the very people who once were its worst enemies. Because of Owens Valley water, Los Angeles grew to the two million population promised by Mulholland. Now the valley's contribution to the city's growth is coming back in the form of tourist dollars. Angelenos, once afraid to identify themselves in the valley, are welcomed as paying customers. Supported by this commerce, Owens Valley today boasts more permanent residents than it did before it came under the shadow of Metropolis. But it is no longer the home of frontier farmers breathing the exhilarating air of self-reliance. It is a tributary province to the city it helped to build.

In addition to his recent Los Angeles: Mission to Modern City, *of which this article forms a part, Remi Nadeau has written three other books on California history, among them* The Water Seekers *(Doubleday, 1950).*

Statement required by the act of August 24, 1912, as amended by the acts of March 3, 1933, July 2, 1946, and June 11, 1960 (74 Stat. 208) showing the ownership, management and circulation of AMERICAN HERITAGE, published bimonthly at New York, N. Y., for October 1, 1961.

1. The names and addresses of the publisher and editor are: Publisher, James Parton; Editor, Oliver Jensen; both of 551 Fifth Avenue, New York 17, N. Y.

2. The owner is: American Heritage Publishing Co., Inc., 551 Fifth Avenue, New York 17, N. Y.; stockholders owning or holding 1 per cent or more of total amount of stock: American Association for State and Local History, Sturbridge, Mass.; The Society of American Historians, Inc., Princeton Library, Princeton, N. J.; Charles Bruce Catton; Irwin Glusker; Oliver O. Jensen; Frank H. Johnson; Richard M. Ketchum; James Parton, individually and as Trustee under Declaration of Trust for James Parton III, dated 12/30/57, as Trustee under Declaration of Trust for Dana Parton, dated 12/30/57, and as Trustee under Declaration of Trust for Agnes L. Parton and a Child of the Grantor, dated 11/15/58; Gerald P. Rosen; Joseph J. Thorndike, Jr., individually and as Trustee under Declaration of Trust for John Thorndike, dated 12/27/57, as Trustee under Declaration of Trust for Alan Thorndike, dated 12/27/57, and as Trustee under Declaration of Trust for Anna Beardsley Lemont, dated 9/15/58; all of 551 Fifth Avenue, New York 17, N. Y.; Richard V. Benson, 301 East 47th Street, New York, N. Y.; Alexander Hehmeyer, 575 Madison Avenue, New York 22, N. Y.; E. F. Hutton & Co. for Margery F. Sachs, 61 Broadway, New York 6, N. Y.; Arnold H. Maremont, 168 North Michigan Avenue, Chicago 1, Ill.; A. J. Ostheimer III, 1510 Chestnut Street, Philadelphia 2, Pa.; E. Michele Phillips, P. O. Box 11, Rowayton, Conn.; Roger S. Phillips, P. O. Box 11, Rowayton, Conn.; Cecily Sachs, c/o Bankers Trust Co., P. O. Box 704, Church St. Station, New York 8, N. Y.; E. J. Stackpole, 220 Telegraph Building, Harrisburg, Pa.; Barbara Joan Straus, 303 St. Pierre Road, Los Angeles 24, California.

3. The known bondholders, mortgagees, and other security holders owning or holding 1 per cent or more of total amount of bonds, mortgages, or other securities are: none.

4. Paragraphs 2 and 3 include, in cases where the stockholder or security holder appears upon the books of the company as trustee or in any other fiduciary relation, the name of the person or corporation for whom such trustee is acting; also the statements in the two paragraphs show the affiant's full knowledge and belief as to the circumstances and conditions under which stockholders and security holders who do not appear upon the books of the company as trustees, hold stock and securities in a capacity other than that of a bona fide owner.

5. The average number of copies of each issue of this publication sold or distributed, through the mails or otherwise, to paid subscribers during the 12 months preceding the date shown above was: 331,410. Signed, James Parton, Publisher. Sworn to and subscribed before me this 6th day of September, 1961. [Seal] Lawrence P. Sweeney, Notary Public (my commission expires March 30, 1962).

Bryan

CONTINUED FROM PAGE 11

Defeat for the Senate did not harm Bryan politically. He was still in his early thirties; to one so young, merely having run for the Senate brought considerable prestige. Also, he had conducted an intelligent and forceful campaign. Even so it was a defeat, certainly not calculated to lead him to the remarkable decision that he made after the Nebraska legislature had turned him down. This decision was to seek nomination for the Presidency of the United States itself!

The young man's "superlative self-assurance" (one might call it effrontery but for the fact that his daring plan succeeded) staggers the imagination. Many men within his party were far better known than he, and his state, Nebraska, was without major influence in Democratic affairs. With Cleveland and the national organization dead-set against free coinage and other inflationary schemes, Bryan's chances of capturing the nomination seemed infinitesimal. But if bold, his action was by no means foolish. Democratic voters were becoming more and more restive under Cleveland's conservative leadership. At least in Bryan's part of the nation, many thoughtful members of the party were beginning to feel that they must look in new directions and find new leaders if they were not to be replaced by the Populists as the country's second major party. Recognizing this situation before most politicians did, Bryan proceeded to act upon his insight with determination and dispatch.

First of all, he set out to make himself known beyond his own locality. Accepting the editorship of the Omaha *World-Herald* at a tiny salary in order to obtain a forum, he turned out a stream of editorials on the silver question, which he sent to influential politicians all over the country. He toured the South and West with his message, speaking everywhere and under all sorts of conditions: to close-packed, cheering throngs and to tiny groups of quiet listeners. His argument was simple but forceful, his oratory magnetic and compelling. Always he made sure to meet local leaders and to subject them to his genial smile, his youthful vigor, his charm, his sincerity. He did not push himself forward; indeed, he claimed to be ready to support any honest man whose program was sound. But he lost no chance to point out to all concerned his own availability. "I don't suppose your delegation is committed to any candidate," he wrote to a prominent Colorado Democrat in April of 1896. "Our delegation may present my name." When the Democratic convention finally met in Chicago, Bryan believed that he was known personally to more of the delegates than any other candidate.

Few delegates took his campaign seriously, however. At the convention, one senator asked Bryan who he thought would win out. Bryan replied characteristically that he believed he himself "had as good a chance to be nominated as anyone," and proceeded to tick off the sources of his strength: Nebraska, "half of the Indian Territory, . . ." but before Bryan could mention his other backers the senator lost interest and walked off with some of his cronies. The candidate, amiable and serene, took no offense. A majority of the delegates favored his position on silver. No one had a clear lead in the race. All he needed was a chance to plead his case.

The opportunity—Bryan called it an "unexpected stroke of luck," although he planned for it brilliantly—came when he was asked to close the debate on the platform's silver plank. When he came forward to address the jam-packed mob in the Chicago auditorium he was tense, but there was a smile on his face, and to observers he seemed the picture of calm self-confidence. He began quietly, but his voice resounded in the farthest corners of the great hall and commanded the attention of every delegate. He was conscious of his own humble position, he told the throng, but he was "clad in the armor of a righteous cause" and this entitled him to speak. As he went on, his tension evaporated and his voice rose. When he recounted the recent history of the struggle between the forces of gold and silver, the audience responded eagerly. "At the close of a sentence," he wrote later, "it would rise and shout, and when I began upon another sentence, the room was still as a church."

He spoke for silver as against gold, for the West over the East, for "the hardy pioneers who have braved all the dangers of the wilderness" as against "the few financial magnates who, in a back room, corner the money of the world."

We have petitioned, and our petitions have been scorned; we have entreated, and our entreaties have been disregarded; we have begged, and they have mocked when our calamity came. We beg no longer; we entreat no more; we petition no more. *We defy them!*

The crowd thundered its agreement. Bryan proceeded. One after another he met the arguments of the party's Cleveland wing head on. Free silver would disturb the business interests? "Gold bugs" were defining the term too narrowly. Remember that wage earners, crossroads merchants, and farmers were also businessmen. The cities favored the gold standard? Their prosperity really depended upon the prosperity of the great agricultural regions of the land, which favored bimetallism.

108

"Burn down your cities and leave our farms," he said, "and your cities will spring up again as if by magic; but destroy our farms and the grass will grow in the streets of every city in the country."

Now Bryan was absolute master of the delegates. "I thought of a choir," he recalled afterward, "as I noted how instantaneously and in unison they responded to each point made." The crowd cheered because he was reflecting its sentiments, but also because it recognized, suddenly, its leader—handsome, confident, righteously indignant, yet also calm, restrained, and ready for responsibility. His mission accomplished, it was time to close, and Bryan had saved a marvelous figure of speech, tested in many an earlier oration, for his climax. "You shall not press down upon the brow of labor this crown of thorns," he warned, bringing his hands down suggestively to his temples; "you shall not crucify mankind upon a cross of gold." Dramatically he extended his arms to the side, the very figure of the crucified Christ.

Amid the hysterical demonstration that followed, it was clear that Bryan had accomplished his miracle. The next day, July 9, he was nominated for the Presidency on the fifth ballot.

The issue was clear-cut, for the Republicans had already declared for the gold standard and nominated the handsome, genial, and thoroughly conservative William McKinley. As a result, the Populists were under great pressure to go along with Bryan. While the Democrats had not adopted all the radical Populist demands, their platform contained a number of liberal planks in addition to that on free silver, including one calling for a federal income tax and another for stiffer controls of the railroad network. For the Populists to insist on nominating a third candidate would simply insure the election of the "gold bug" McKinley. Not every important Populist favored fusion; some were ready to concede defeat in 1896 and build their party for the future on broadly radical lines. "The Democratic idea of fusion," said Tom Watson of Georgia angrily, is "that we play Jonah while they play whale." But the rich scent of victory in the air was too much for the majority to resist. "I care not for party names," said "Sockless Jerry" Simpson bluntly; "it is the substance we are after, and we have it in William J. Bryan." Indeed, Bryan's friendly association with the Populists in earlier campaigns and his essentially Populistic views on most questions made it difficult for the party to oppose him. "We put him to school," one anti-Bryan Populist later remarked, "and he wound up by stealing the school-books." In any case, the Populist convention endorsed him; thus the silver forces united to do battle with the Republicans.

THE CONTROVERSIAL COMMONER

CULVER PICTURES

When McKeighan died [William McKeighan, Nebraska free-silverite], Bryan came down to the sun-scorched, dried-up, blown-away little village of Red Cloud to speak at his funeral. There, with an audience of some few hundreds of bronzed farmers who believed in him as their deliverer, the man who could lead them out of the bondage of debt, who could stay the drought and strike water from the rock, I heard him make the greatest speech of his life. Surely that was eloquence of the old stamp that was accounted divine, eloquence that reached through the callus of ignorance and toil and found and awoke the stunted souls of men. I saw those rugged men of the soil weep like children. Six months later, at Chicago, when Bryan stampeded a convention, appropriated a party, electrified a nation . . . one of those ragged farmers sat beside me in the gallery, and at the close of that never-to-be-forgotten speech, he leaned over the rail, the tears on his furrowed cheeks, and shouted, "The sweet singer of Israel."
—*Willa Cather, in* Round-up: A Nebraska Reader

What a disgusting, dishonest fakir Bryan is! When I see so many Americans running after him, I feel very much as I do when a really lovely woman falls in love with a cad.
—*Elihu Root to William M. Laffan, October 31, 1900*

As for Bryan, though he has many kindly and amiable traits, what a shallow demagogue he is! I do not believe he is a bit worse than Thomas Jefferson, and I do not think that if elected President he will be a worse President. The country would survive, but it would suffer just as the country suffered for at least two generations because of its folly in following Jefferson's lead.
—*Theodore Roosevelt to Henry Cabot Lodge, August 6, 1906*

It has become the custom nowadays, among supercilious people, to depict Bryan as a clown, or a fool, or a mountebank. He was nothing of the kind. In many respects, he was one of the shrewdest men I have ever known. In him, unsophistication and sagacity were strangely blended. Along with this he was truthful and square. His friendships were sincere; one could depend implicitly on his word. . . . He turned every public question into a moral issue. He was by nature a crusader, a reformer. . . . But anyone who pictures him as a grumpy, sour, muddled fanatic is wholly wrong. . . .

As I think of him there comes into my mind what somebody said of Gladstone—that to keep hating him, one had to avoid meeting him. I cannot say if this was true of Gladstone, but it was certainly true of William Jennings Bryan.
—*William G. McAdoo, in* Crowded Years

Both Bryan and McKinley men realized at once that this was to be a close and crucial contest. Seldom have the two great parties divided so clearly on fundamental issues; a showdown was inevitable; a major turning point in American history had been reached. Silver against gold was but the surface manifestation of the struggle. City against countryside, industry against agriculture, East against South and West, the nineteenth century against the twentieth—these were the real contestants in 1896.

After Bryan's nomination McKinley's manager, Mark Hanna, abandoned plans for a vacation cruise in New England waters and plunged into the work of the campaign. The situation was "alarming," he told McKinley. A "communistic spirit" was abroad, business was "all going to pieces." A mighty effort was called for. Hanna raised huge sums by "assessing" the great bankers, oil refiners, insurance men, and meat packers, using the threat of impending business chaos and wild inflation to loosen the purse strings of the tycoons. While McKinley, "the advance agent of prosperity," conducted a dignified and carefully organized campaign from his front porch in Canton, Ohio (*see* "The Front Porch Campaign," AMERICAN HERITAGE, December, 1959), 1,400 paid speakers beat the bushes for votes in every doubtful district. The Republican campaign committee distributed more than 120,000,000 pieces of literature printed in ten languages to carry its message to the voters. Boiler-plate editorials and other releases were sent free to hundreds of small-town newspapers. Hanna, Theodore Roosevelt said, "has advertised McKinley as if he were a patent medicine!" The Republican organization reached a peak of efficiency and thoroughness never before approached in a political contest; the campaign marked a methodological revolution that has profoundly affected every presidential contest since.

Bryan had little money, and no organizational genius like Hanna to direct his drive. But he too effected a revolution that has left its mark on modern campaigning. McKinley's front porch technique was novel only in the huge number of visiting delegations that Hanna paraded across his man's lawn and the exaggerated care that the candidate took to avoid saying anything impolitic. It had always been considered undignified for a presidential nominee to go out and hunt for votes on his own. Bryan cast off this essentially hypocritical tradition at the very start. He realized that the concerted power of business and the press were aligned against him, and that his own greatest assets were his magnificent ability as a political orator and his personal sincerity and charm. His opponent could afford to sit tight; *he* must seek out the people everywhere if they were to receive his message. Between summer and November he traveled a precedent-shattering 18,000 miles, making more than 600 speeches and addressing directly an estimated 5,000,000 Americans. His secretary estimated that he uttered between 60,000 and 100,000 words every day during the campaign.

On the stump he was superb. Without straining his voice he could make himself heard to a restless open-air throng numbered in the tens of thousands. He was equally effective at the whistle stops, outlining his case from the rear platform of his train while a handful of country people gazed earnestly upward from the roadbed. He was unfailingly pleasant and unpretentious. At one stop, while he was shaving in his compartment, a small group outside the train began clamoring for a glimpse of him. Flinging open the window and beaming through the lather, he cheerfully shook hands with each of these admirers. Neither he nor they, according to the recorder of this incident, saw anything unusual or undignified in the performance. Thousands of well-wishers sent him good luck charms and messages of encouragement. "If the people who have given me rabbits' feet in this campaign will vote for me, there is no possible doubt of my election," he said in one speech. It was because of this simple friendliness that he became known as "the Great Commoner."

Bryan was also unfailingly interesting. Even his most unsympathetic biographer admits that he spoke so well that at every stop the baggagemen from the campaign train would run back to listen to his talk—and this despite a schedule that called for as many as thirty speeches a day.

Such a campaign is an effective means of projecting an image of a candidate and his general point of view. It is not well suited for the making of complicated arguments and finely drawn distinctions; for that the McKinley approach was far superior. Wisely, for it was clearly the issue uppermost in the minds of most voters, Bryan hammered repeatedly at the currency question. He did not avoid talking about other matters: he attacked the railroads and the great business monopolists and the "tyranny" of the eastern bankers. He deplored the use of militia in labor disputes and of the injunction as a means of breaking strikes. He spoke in favor of income taxes, higher wages, and relief for hard-pressed mortgagees. But the silver issue was symbolic, and the Democratic position sound. There *was* a currency shortage; deflation *was* injuring millions of debtors and pouring a rich unearned increment into the pockets of bondholders. To say, as Henry Demarest Lloyd did at the time and as many liberal historians have since, that Bryan made free silver the "cowbird" of the reform movement, pushing out all other issues from the reform nest and thus destroying them, is an exaggeration and a distortion. All effective politicians stick to a small number of simple issues while on the stump; otherwise, in the hectic conflict of a hot campaign, they project no message at all. There is no reason to suspect that, if elected, Bryan would have forgotten about other reform measures and concentrated only on the currency.

For a time Bryan's gallant, singlehanded battle seemed to be having an effect on public opinion, and Republican leaders became thoroughly frightened. In addition to money, threats and imprecations now became weapons in the campaign. A rumor was circulated that Bryan was insane. The *New York Times* devoted columns to the possibility, and printed a letter from a supposed psychologist charging that he was suffering from "paranoia querulenta," "graphomania," and "oratorical monomania." "Men," one manufacturer told his workers, "vote as you please, but if Bryan is elected . . . the whistle will not blow Wednesday morning." According to the *Nation*, which was supporting McKinley, many companies placed orders with their suppliers "to be executed in case Mr. Bryan is defeated, and not otherwise." A Chicago company that held thousands of farm mortgages politely asked all its "customers" to indicate their presidential preferences—a not very subtle form of coercion but probably an effective one. In some cases men were actually fired because of their political opinions.

By the time election day arrived the McKinley managers were so confident of victory that Hanna began returning new contributions as no longer necessary. Nevertheless, a final monumental effort was made to get out the vote. Free transportation was provided to carry citizens to and from the polls, men were paid for time lost in voting, and in doubtful districts floaters and other disreputables were rounded up and paraded to the ballot boxes. Everywhere in the crucial North Central states the Hanna machine expended enormous efforts, and in these states the decision was made. McKinley carried them all and with them the nation. In the electoral college McKinley won by 271 to 176, but the popular vote was close—7,036,000 to 6,468,000. The change of a relative handful of votes in half a dozen key states would have swung the election to Bryan.

The victory, however, was McKinley's, and conservatives all over America—and the world—echoed the sentiment of Hanna's happy telegram to the President-elect: GOD'S IN HIS HEAVEN, ALL'S RIGHT WITH THE WORLD! A watershed in the economic and social history of the United States had been crossed. The rural America of the nineteenth century was making way for the industrial America of the twentieth. Soon business conditions began to improve, agricultural prices inched upward, new discoveries of gold relieved the pressure on the money supply. While McKinley and Hanna (now senator from Ohio) ruled in Washington, the era of complacent materialism and easy political virtue that had entered American politics on the coattails of General Grant seemed destined to continue indefinitely. Reform, it appeared, was dead.

That these appearances were deceiving was due in considerable measure to William Jennings Bryan. Unchastened by defeat and always cheerful ("It is better to have run and lost than never to have run at all," he said), he maintained the leadership of his party. Consistently he took the liberal position on important issues. Despite his strong pacifism he approved of fighting Spain in 1898 in order to free Cuba. "Humanity demands that we should act," he said simply. He enlisted in the Army and rose to be a colonel, although he saw no action during the brief conflict. The sincerity of his motives was proved when the war ended, for he then fought against the plan to annex former Spanish colonies. Running for President a second time in 1900, he made resistance to imperialism an issue in the campaign along with free silver. If both of these were poorly calculated to win votes in 1900, they were nonetheless solidly in the liberal tradition. Bryan lost to McKinley again, this time by 861,459 votes, and leadership of the reform movement passed, after McKinley's assassination, to Theodore Roosevelt. But Bryan continued the fight. In 1904, battling almost alone against conservatives in his own party, he forced the adoption of a fairly liberal platform (including strong antitrust, pro-labor, and antitariff planks), and when the conservative Judge Alton B. Parker was nonetheless nominated for President, Bryan kept up his outspoken criticism. While remaining loyal to the Democratic party he announced boldly: "The fight on economic questions . . . is not abandoned. As soon as the election is over I shall . . . organize for the campaign of 1908."

In that campaign Bryan, once more the Democratic nominee, was once more defeated in his personal quest of the Presidency, this time by Roosevelt's handpicked successor, William Howard Taft. Immediately he announced that he would not seek the office again, thus throwing the field open to other liberals.

Although he thus abandoned formal leadership of the Democrats, Bryan continued to advocate reform. Throughout the Taft administration he campaigned up and down the country to bolster the liberal wing of his party. When the 1912 nominating convention met in Baltimore, he introduced and won approval of a highly controversial resolution denouncing Wall Street influence, and he stated repeatedly that he would not support any candidate who was under the slightest obligation to Tammany Hall. The platform, as one historian says, "was a progressive document, in the best Bryan tradition." In the end Bryan threw his support to Woodrow Wilson. While this alone did not account for Wilson's nomination, it was very important in his election, for it assured him the enthusiastic backing of millions of loyal Bryanites.

Nothing reveals Bryan's fine personal qualities better than his support of Wilson, for the former Princeton professor had opposed the Great Commoner since 1896, when he had called the Cross of Gold speech "ridiculous." In 1904 he had publicly demanded that the Bryan wing be "utterly and once and for all driven from Democratic counsels." As late as 1908 he had refused to appear on the same platform with Bryan. Mr. Bryan, he said, "is the most charming and lovable of men personally, but foolish and dangerous in his theoretical beliefs." During the campaign of that year he refused to allow Bryan to deliver a campaign speech on the Princeton campus.

By 1912 Wilson had become far more liberal and no longer opposed most of Bryan's policies; even so, had Bryan been a lesser man he would not have forgiven these repeated criticisms. But he was more concerned with Wilson's 1912 liberalism than with personal matters, despite the publication of an old letter in which Wilson had expressed the wish to "knock Mr. Bryan once and for all into a cocked hat!" He shrugged off the "cocked hat" letter, and when Wilson paid him a handsome public tribute they became good friends. Furthermore, during the 1912 campaign, Bryan campaigned vigorously for Wilson, making well over four hundred speeches within a period of seven weeks. When Wilson won an easy victory in November, Bryan reacted without a trace of envy or bitterness. "It is a great triumph," he declared, "Let every Democratic heart rejoice." A few months later he said in a speech in Chicago:

Sometimes I have had over-sanguine friends express regret that I did not reach the presidency. . . . But I have an answer ready for them. I have told them that they need not weep for me. . . . I have been so much more interested in the securing of the things for which we have been fighting than I have been in the name of the man who held the office, that I am happy in the thought that this government, through these reforms, will be made so good that a citizen will not miss a little thing like the presidency.

Wilson made Bryan Secretary of State. He was needed in the administration to help manage his many friends in Congress. The strategy worked well, for Bryan used his influence effectively. His role was particularly crucial in the hard fight over the Federal Reserve bill, but his loyal aid was also important in

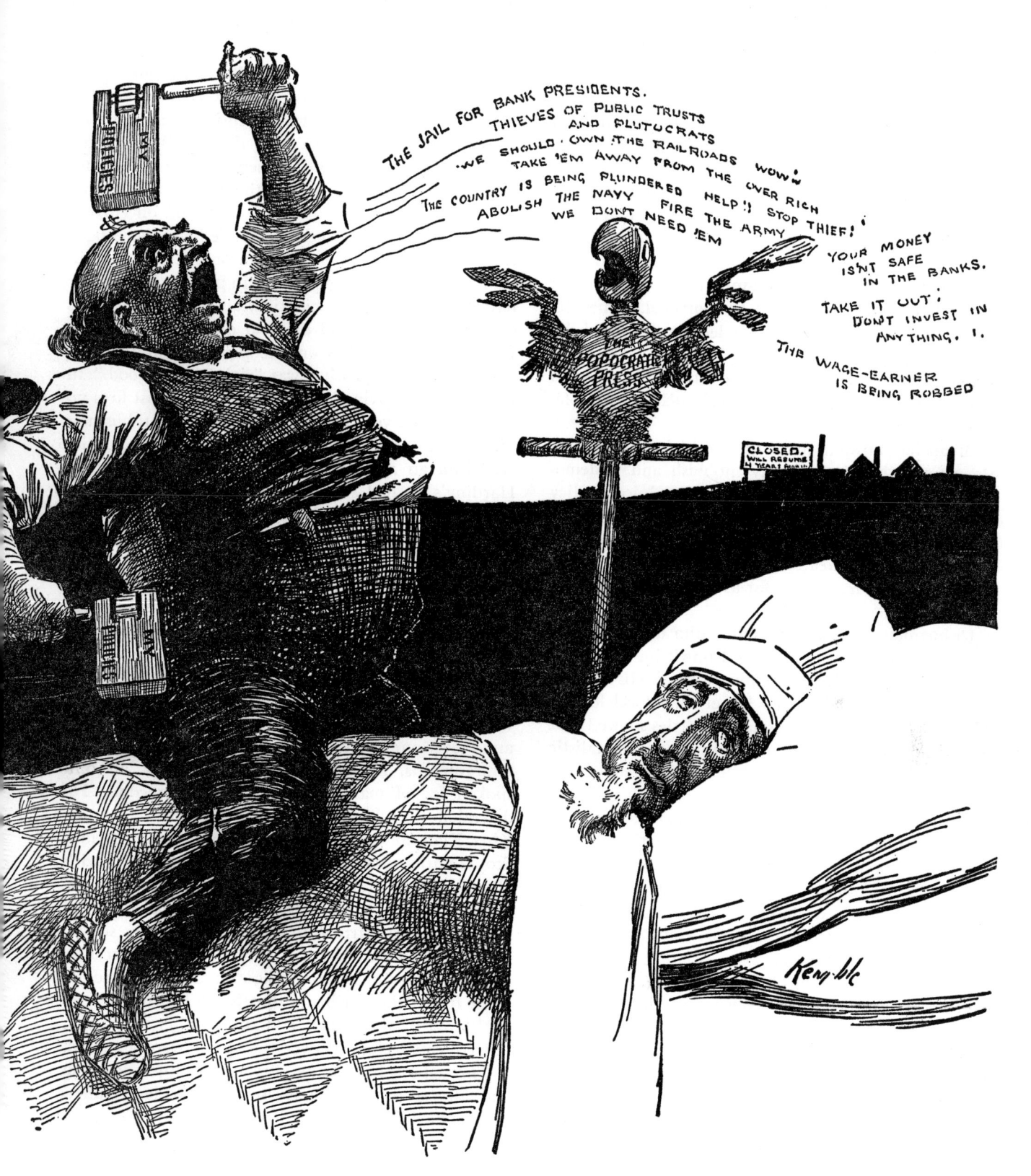

WHAT FOUR YEARS OF BRYAN WOULD MEAN

UNCLE SAM. "IF SOMEBODY WOULD ONLY CHLOROFORM HIM, AND LET ME HAVE A MUCH-NEEDED REST"

Harper's Weekly, OCT. 10, 1908; CULVER PICTURES

passing income tax legislation and a new antitrust law and in other matters as well.

In managing foreign affairs Bryan was less successful, for in this field he was ill-prepared. Because of his frank belief in the spoils system, he dismissed dozens of key professional diplomats, replacing them with untrained political hacks. Naturally the Foreign Service was badly injured. His policy of not serving alcoholic beverages at official functions because of his personal convictions caused much criticism at home and abroad. "W. J. Bryan not only suffers for his principles and mortifies his flesh, as he has every right to do," the London *Daily Express* complained, "but he insists that others should suffer and be mortified." The Secretary's continuing Chautauqua lectures, at which he sometimes appeared on the same platform with vaudeville entertainers and freaks, were attacked by many as undignified for one who occupied such a high official position.

Bryan had answers to all these criticisms: the State Department had been overly snobbish and undemocratic; Wilson had agreed to his "grape juice" policy before appointing him; no one should be ashamed of speaking to the American people. He could also point to his "cooling-off treaties" with some twenty nations, which provided machinery for avoiding blow-ups over minor diplomatic imbroglios.

Unfortunately Bryan had but a dim understanding of Latin American problems and unwittingly fostered American imperialism on many occasions. His narrow-minded belief that he knew better than local leaders what was "good" for these small countries showed that he had no comprehension of cultural and nationalistic elements in other lands. Although well intended, his policies produced much bad feeling in South and Central America. Bryan did suggest lending Latin American nations money "for education, sanitation and internal development," a policy that anticipated our modern Point Four approach to underdeveloped areas. Wilson, however, dismissed the idea because he thought it "would strike the whole country . . . as a novel and radical proposal."

When the World War broke out in 1914, Bryan, like his chief, adopted a policy of strict neutrality. America, he said, should attempt to mediate between the belligerents by suggesting "a more rational basis of peace." Bryan believed in real neutrality far more deeply than Wilson, who was not ready to face the possibility of a German victory. "We cannot have in mind the wishes of one side more than the wishes of the other side," Bryan warned the President after the latter had prepared a stiff note of protest against German submarine warfare. And when, after the sinking of the *Lusitania,* Wilson sent a series of threatening messages to Germany, Bryan resigned as Secretary of State. He never again held public office.

It would have been better for Bryan's reputation if he had died in 1915; instead he lived on for another decade, as amiable and well-intentioned as ever but increasingly out of touch with the rapidly changing times. He made no effort to keep up with the abrupt intellectual developments of the twentieth century, yet he was accustomed to speak his mind on current issues and continued to do so. There had always been those who had considered his uncomplicated faith in time-tested moral principles and in popular rule rather naïve; in the cynical, scientific, and amoral twenties only a relative handful of rural oldtimers saw much virtue in his homilies on the people's unfailing instinct to do always what was "right" and "good." In the world of Calvin Coolidge the old Populist fires no longer burned very brightly, and Bryan's anti-business bias seemed terribly old-fashioned. Many had considered him an anachronism even in Wilson's day; by Harding's he had simply ceased to count in politics. More and more he confined himself to religious questions. His ardent piety was heartwarming, but he was a smug and intolerant Fundamentalist whose ignorance of modern science and ethics did not prevent him from expounding his "views" on these subjects at length. The honest opinions of "the people," he believed, could "settle" scientific and philosophical questions as easily as political ones.

Advancing age, as well as increasing preoccupation with revealed religion, was making Bryan less tolerant. Never one to give much thought to reasoned counterarguments, he became, in the twenties, an outspoken foe of many aspects of human freedom. He defended prohibition, refused to condemn the Ku Klux Klan, and participated eagerly in the notorious Scopes anti-evolution trial in Dayton, Tennessee, with all its overtones of censorship and self-satisfied ignorance. The final great drama of Bryan's life occurred when Clarence Darrow mercilessly exposed his simple prejudices on the witness stand. Bryan complacently maintained, among other things, that Eve was actually made from Adam's rib and that Jonah had really been swallowed by the whale. The rural audience cheered, but educated men all over the world were appalled.

Throughout his lifetime, Bryan was subject to harsh and almost continual criticism, and at least superficially he failed in nearly everything he attempted. But he was too secure in his faith to be injured by criticism, and he knew that for over two decades his influence was greater than any of his contemporaries save Theodore Roosevelt and Wilson. His life was useful and happy, for he rightly believed that he had made a lasting contribution to his country's development. Nor is it fair to condemn him for his limited intelligence and superficial understanding of his times. Other political leaders of at best ordinary intellect have done great deeds, sometimes without appreciating the meaning of events they have helped to shape. Still, there was tragedy in Bryan's career—he was unable to grow.

In 1896 he was indeed the peerless leader, vital, energetic, dedicated, and, in a measure, imaginative. He saw the problems of Nebraska farmers, realized their wider implications, and outlined a reasonable program designed to deal with them. He was almost elected President as a result, despite his youth and inexperience. Suddenly he was a celebrity; thereafter he moved into a wider world and lived there at his ease. He did not abandon his principles, and he helped achieve many important reforms, for which we must always honor him, but he soon ceased to feed upon new ideas. In a sense, despite the defeats, life's rewards came to him too easily. His magnetic voice, his charm, his patent sincerity, the memory of the heroic fight of '96—these things secured his place and relieved him of the need to grapple with new concepts.

Although he was a man of courage, strength, and endurance, Bryan was essentially lax and complacent. He preferred baggy clothes, a full stomach, the easy, undemanding companionship of small minds. For years the momentum of 1896 carried him on, but eventually the speeding world left him far behind. Fortunately for his inner well-being, he never realized what had happened. A few days after Darrow had exposed his shallowness before the world, he died peacefully in his sleep, as serene and unruffled by events as ever.

John A. Garraty is a professor of history at Columbia University and a frequent contributor to AMERICAN HERITAGE.

For further reading: The Memoirs of William Jennings Bryan by Himself and His Wife, Mary Baird Bryan *(John C. Winston, 1925);* The Trumpet Soundeth, *by Paul W. Glad (University of Nebraska Press, 1960);* The Peerless Leader, William Jennings Bryan, *by Paxton Hibben (Farrar & Rinehart, 1929).*

WILSON ON DEMOCRACY

What is democracy that it should be possible, nay natural, to some nations, impossible as yet to others? Why has it been a cordial and a tonic to little Switzerland and to big America, while it has been as yet only a quick intoxicant or a slow poison to France and Spain, a mere maddening draught to the South American states? Why has England approached democratic institutions by slow and steady stages of deliberate and peaceful development, while so many other states have panted towards democracy through constant revolution? Why has democracy existed in America and in Australia virtually from the first, while other states have utterly failed in every effort to establish it? . . .

Democracy is of course wrongly conceived when treated as merely a body of doctrine, or as simply a form of government. It is a stage of development. It is not created by aspirations or by new faith: it is built up by slow habit. Its process is experience, its basis old wont, its meaning national organic unity and effectual life. It comes, like manhood, as the fruit of youth: immature peoples cannot have it, and the maturity to which it is vouchsafed is the maturity of freedom and self-control, and no other. It is conduct, and its only stable foundation is character. America has democracy because she is free; she is not free because she has democracy. A particular form of government may no more be adopted than a particular type of character may be adopted: both institutions and character must be developed by conscious effort and through transmitted aptitudes. The variety of effects produced by democratic principles, therefore, upon different nations and systems, and even upon the same nation at different periods, is susceptible of instructive explanation. It is not the result of accident merely, nor of good fortune, manifestly, that the English race has been the only race, outside of quiet, closeted Switzerland, the only race, that is, standing forward amidst the fierce contests of national rivalries, that has succeeded in establishing and maintaining the most liberal forms of government. It is, on the contrary, a perfectly natural outcome of organic development. The English alone have approached popular institutions *through habit.* All other races have rushed prematurely into them through mere impatience with habit: have adopted democracy, instead of cultivating it. . . .

There is really, when American institutions are compared with English, nothing essentially novel in our political arrangements: they are simply the normal institutions of the Englishman in America. They are, in other words, English institutions as modified by the conditions surrounding settlements effected under corporate charters, in separate but neighbor colonies; above all as dominated by the material, economic, and social conditions attending the advance of the race in America. These conditions it is, not political principles, that have controlled our intellectual as well as our political development.

—*Woodrow Wilson, 1889*

READING, WRITING, AND HISTORY

By BRUCE CATTON

Pioneers at Sea

The story of America, we frequently remind ourselves, is the story of the conquest of a continent. It begins at Jamestown, at Plymouth, or wherever one chooses, and goes through forests, mountains, and prairies all the way to the sunset; and it shows a restless, acquisitive, and usually indomitable breed of men converting an immense stretch of land to the uses of a large, energetic, and intricately organized society. The pioneer of course is the hero, complete with such artifacts as the axe, the long rifle, and the covered wagon, going west with prodigious strides, followed presently by the promoter, the sturdy artisan, and the far-seeing man of business. It is a fabulous story, and we could recite it in our sleep.

What we sometimes overlook is the fact that before the pioneer could conquer this continent, he first had to cross the ocean. After he had crossed it and settled down to his wilderness-taming, he had to get supplies from the old country, find markets there for the products he was wresting from the new land, make money enough to finance further pioneering, and arrange for a sea-borne transportation system that would intimately link this new country with the larger, older, and wealthier countries beyond the seas. He had to conquer the oceans, in other words, as well as the land, and his salt-water pioneering was as important as anything he did ashore. Along with his seven-league boots he had to have webfeet.

This restatement of the obvious is evoked by Carl C. Cutler's excellent new book, *Queens of the Western Ocean,* which shows how an important part of that deep-sea pioneering was accomplished and what it meant to America.

Mr. Cutler addresses himself chiefly to one aspect: the establishment of regular, scheduled lines of sailing vessels connecting the eastern seaports with England and Europe, and the simultaneous creation of scheduled lines running along the American coast, all the way from New England to Louisiana. Here, he remarks, was one of the most significant chapters in American history. It was a short chapter, running through forty-odd years up to 1860; after that the nation focused its attention on shoreside matters and let someone else do its sea-borne carrying. But while it lasted it represented the extension of a discovery made early in the game—that the colonies, like the young republic which grew out of them, had to build and control their own merchant marine if they were going to prosper.

The going was tough. In the colonial period there were restrictive laws designed to keep colonial trade in the hands of British shippers. There were extensive wars, during which naval cruisers and privateers harried the sea lanes; and at all times American vessels had to compete with bigger, richer, better-established shipping firms overseas. As a result—whether he was dodging the king's revenue cutters, getting away from sea raiders, or simply trying to beat his rival into the market—the American sailor had to have a fast ship. The design had to be good, and the seamanship had to be superb. Right from the beginning, the American merchant mariner learned to put a high value on a speedy passage.

It paid off. The growing merchant fleet, made up for the most part of small vesssels but handled by canny traders with the acutest competitive instincts, found markets for American exports, and—Mr. Cutler insists—actually served to finance a good part of the development of the new nation. By the time the War of 1812 was out of the way and the world at last was at peace, America was ready for deep-sea trade on a large scale. The nation had a big surplus of exportable surpluses, and Europe had war-emptied warehouses waiting to receive them. Also, there were increasing numbers of immigrants eager to take ship for the United States.

There were boom times for a couple of years, then there was a recession. The surpluses had been exported, Europe's most pressing needs had been met, and during the boom the merchant fleet had been overbuilt. By 1817 the trader had to scratch for what he could get. It was time for really sharp competition.

Out of this came the packet lines. The first of these, the famous Black Ball line of sailing ships between New York and Liverpool, was based on the idea that it would pay to compete for the high-priced trade—passengers, and package merchandise. The competition would be based on something new under the sun: ships that would sail on regular, established dates, whether or not they had filled their holds.

It sounds simple now: that is the way all ships go. But nobody had ever done it before. A ship would be posted to go from New York to Liverpool, and it would lie at its wharf, week after week, passengers fretting unavailingly, until at last it had a cargo, and then it would leave. Here, for the first time, was a fixed schedule. A traveler could say, "I am going to leave next

---

Queens of the Western Ocean, by Carl C. Cutler, with a foreword by Chester W. Nimitz. United States Naval Institute. 672 pp. $12.50.

Friday," and next Friday he would leave, no matter how slowly his ship might go. It was revolutionary . . . and, after a few hard years, it paid.

It paid so well that many other lines followed, giving birth to the expression, "ocean liner." There were regular schedules everywhere—from American ports to England and Europe, and from one American port to another American port; ships were made larger and faster, they were driven harder and harder, and a successful packet captain was a public figure of renown. The passenger had a chance—for the first time—to travel in something like comfort. Staterooms previously had been pigeonholes, five feet high and six by six; now they had modern dimensions and livability, and their occupants were not compelled to have a Spartan attitude toward life.

This coincided with the period of America's great growth and development; it was part of it, and it contributed measurably to it. As Mr. Cutler remarks, the vision, daring, and resourcefulness of these sailing-ship men "advanced by many years the financial and industrial growth of the nation, and, in addition, provided the funds to purchase the vast territories that now comprise two thirds of its area." Steam caught up with them, to be sure, in the 1850's. The very demand for regularity and speed which they had evoked made their ships and their skills out of date, at last, and the sailing packet became one with the Phoenician galley. But it was a great day while it lasted.

The Racing Machines

The climactic years of sail were spectacular all along the line. In addition to devising transatlantic vessels which for a time held their own with steam, American designers and traders brought out the Cape Horn clippers, the inexpressibly beautiful ships that set unimaginable speed records and captured men's imaginations as no other form of transportation has ever done. The clippers were highly uneconomic, as cargo carriers, and they flowered only during a brief time when special conditions prevailed in two or three long-distance trade routes, but while they lasted they were something special.

Many people have written about them, in the century since they disappeared forever, but the classic is still Mr. Cutler's *Greyhounds of the Sea,* originally issued in 1930 and brought out now as a companion volume to *Queens of the Western Ocean.* It covers some of the same ground that is covered in the more recent book, but it centers most of its attention on the flyers which briefly crowded the British out of the China tea trade, cut a month or more off the ordinary time between New York and San Francisco, and raised the general prestige of the American merchant ship to the highest point it ever reached.

Mr. Cutler emphasizes a point worth remembering. The greatest of the clippers were only in part a matter of successful design. The design was there, to be sure, and the business of shaping a hull so that the wind could take it through the water with great speed was understood perfectly by such men as John W. Griffiths, Donald McKay, and William H. Webb. But the skipper was equally important, if not a little more so. The clippers had to be driven to the very limit of their capacity by men who understood seamanship down to its last obscure footnote. They needed expert handling precisely as a racing automobile needs it; and they got it from sea captains who had been trained in the packets, in the down-Easters, in the cotton carriers, and the China traders. As Mr. Cutler remarks, such sailors as Robert Waterman and Nathaniel B. Palmer would have made a fair clipper-ship era all by themselves

---

Greyhounds of the Sea, by Carl C. Cutler, with a foreword by Charles Francis Adams. United States Naval Institute. 592 pp. $12.50.

---

regardless of the vessels they commanded. They and a few more like them were men who knew, by instinct and by hard experience, precisely how to drive a ship to the outer margin of safety without ever going beyond it. It is probable that no men ever lived who understood sailing better than they did.

It was the gold-rush era in California that really brought the clipper ship to its peak. Just when the old mania for making fast passages had produced incomparable ships and men who knew how to handle them, boom times on the west coast created a temporarily insatiable desire for vessels that could take passengers and freight out to San Francisco in the shortest possible time. The clippers responded in a dazzling manner. Average sailing-ship time from New York to the Golden Gate had run between 175 and 200 days. The clippers cut this down to 120, then to 110. A few made the trip in less than one hundred days, and two—the famous *Flying Cloud,* and the *Andrew Jackson*—did it in eighty-nine. The *Sea Witch,* which already had set the all-time speed record for the trip from China to New York, got out to San Francisco in ninety-seven days; the *Flying Fish* did it in ninety-two, after losing three mortal days in calms within one hundred miles of the Golden Gate.

To go from New York to San Francisco in three months does not sound very exciting now, when a jet plane can make the trip between lunch time and dinner time and a transcontinental train can get its passengers across the continent in surpassing comfort over a weekend; but in the 1850's it was nothing less than fabulous. For a few brief years it looked—to sailing-ship enthusiasts, at least—as if the windjammer had provided its own answer to the challenge of the steamship. Not for a generation would a steamer equal the clipper *Lightning*'s run of 436 nautical miles in twenty-four hours. (The mark was beaten by two other clippers, however—the *Marco Polo* and the *Champion of the Seas.*)

The golden age was short, but while it lasted it put an indelible streak of color in the record of the American merchant marine. What men thought of the clippers is evident from the names they gave them—*Herald of the Morning, Surprise, Sovereign of the Seas, Twilight, Flying Cloud, Young America, Shooting Star, Northern Light;* the list is a long one, the names coming off like poetry. The wholly prosaic business of carrying cargo from one port to another briefly entered a new dimension and became a reaching out for perfection itself.

It ended almost as quickly as it had begun. By 1855 the boom was over, and some of the world's fastest ships lay idle at the wharves, waiting for freight. They were racing machines, after all, costly to build and costly to operate, and they gave way before long to bulkier vessels which carried larger cargoes more cheaply and more slowly. One great difficulty was that the hard driving which the clippers were given racked them to pieces. Their lives were short; the ones which survived had their sail plans drastically cut down and thereafter sailed more humbly and sedately. Mr. Cutler points out that no one who did not see the clippers before 1860 ever saw them in all their glory. They were like Samson after his haircut. Many of them were still in service, but the old magic was gone. The unusual economic conditions which made the clippers pay did not last very long. When those conditions vanished, so did the flyers. The national intensity of purpose which had created them found different objectives—the internal development of the country, and then the terrible quarrel that led to the Civil War. America was turning away from the sea.

The Shanghai Passage

It remains to make one more point which is essential to any attempt to understand the heyday and the long decline of the American sailing ship. It was a time which was very hard on the ships themselves, but it was infinitely harder on the men who sailed them. The foremast hands who took those winged racers so far and so fast were driven much more mercilessly than the ships they manned. The skippers and mates of the packets and the Cape Horners were, as noted, consummate seamen, but they also bore a strong resemblance to Simon Legree. They ruled with belaying pins and knuckledusters, and the human costs of their achievements were often sickening.

One reason was, quite simply, that the supply of willing seamen had run out. The sailor's life, at best, was hard, and young Americans were quitting the sea for easier, better-paid jobs ashore just when the clipper-ship era was getting started. The captains had to take what they could get when they made up their crews, and increasingly what they could get was the sweepings of the seaports, ne'er-do-wells, landsmen who hardly knew one end of a ship from the other, men who went to sea, in a sense, in spite of themselves. Quite literally, the captain who wanted to make a fast passage and keep his ship afloat had to beat these men into shape.

Even more important was the fact that during its final half-century the deepwater windjammer was fighting a losing fight economically, a matter which became even more pressing after the clippers had vanished. The sailing ship of the latter half of the nineteenth century had to operate on the cheap, and in the last analysis this meant that it could operate only by exploiting its crews to the very limit. The "bucko mate," who ruled by unadulterated brutality, was a necessity, and the name "hell ship" was attached to one after another of the vessels that struggled to compete with steam. Rarely in the world's history have supposedly free men been so evilly handled as were the crews of the last windjammers.

There is a detailed account of how this worked and what it meant in Richard H. Dillon's *Shanghaiing Days*, a somewhat disorganized and poorly assembled book which does shed a graphic light on the almost incredible conditions under which men went to sea in the last days of sail. It belongs with Mr. Cutler's books: they show the beauty and the romance; this one shows the dark underside, a useful and shocking corrective to the picturesque accounts of noble ships and dauntless skippers.

To begin with, the sailor was wholly at the mercy of the waterfront crimp, an antisocial character who infested the seaports and got a monopoly on the business of supplying sailing ships with sailors. The waterfront boardinghouses which the sailor automatically headed for when his ship paid off were run by the crimps who separated the sailor from his money as rapidly as possible, got him into debt, and then signed him up for a new voyage, cashed his advance note, and shipped him off to sea.

At its best, this was a bad deal. The sailor tolerated it, partly because there was not very much he could do about it—if he wanted to get another ship, he had to get it through the crimps, who controlled the hiring—and partly because he could usually count on a couple of weeks of gaudy carousing of the kind traditional for seafaring men from time immemorial. But the business was not at its best very often. For the crimp developed a way of giving his man one night's binge and then either getting him dead drunk or feeding him knockout drops (which was simpler and cheaper) and promptly delivering his inert carcass aboard some deepwater ship that was just about to sail. The sailor would come to, with aching head, to find that he was off on another long cruise on some ship he had never heard of before.

This was the famous "Shanghai passage," invented apparently in San Francisco but widely copied. As the pressure for men grew stronger, the crimp reached out for non-sailors, and there were times and places when any man who entered a waterfront saloon did so at his dire peril—he might wake up in a squalid forecastle, completely at the mercy of a captain and a mate who would kick and club him into performance of dangerous and unfamiliar tasks.

The shipping firms, both American and British, put up with this because it paid. When crimps persuaded sailors to desert a ship—and they were expert at this task, promising men anxious to get off a "hell ship" all sorts of shoreside jobs—the money that was due those men in wages did not have to be paid. When a

---

Shanghaiing Days, by Richard H. Dillon. Coward-McCann, Inc. 352 pp. $4.75.

---

new crew was to be hired, to be sure, the crimp had to get his blood money, but the fees were deducted from the pay the new hands would earn.

Mr. Dillon examines this business in all of its dreadful detail, coupling his recital of the horrendous things that were done to sailors ashore with a description of the equally horrendous things that were done to them afloat. The story is simply incredible, or would be if it were not so amply documented. The whole thing is a stain on the American record, and it leaves one with the feeling that the sailing ship did not go out of existence too soon.

This exploitation did finally come to an end, of course. Public opinion was at length revolted and laws were passed. The sailing ship gave way to the steamer, and the crimp's place in the picture automatically declined. Also, the sailors finally got a union and were able to do something in the way of asserting their rights. In the end—somewhere in the early 1900's—the sorry old system died out.

One of the men who helped to kill it was a sailor named Andrew Furuseth, who helped to establish the union which the sailors needed. Furuseth once summed up conditions on the old sailing ships as neatly as any man could. Arrested after some organizing fracas on the docks, he was sentenced to jail, and he remarked that he did not mind very much—no jail, he said, could possibly give him worse living quarters, worse food, or more inhuman treatment than he was used to on shipboard.

A Civil War Proposal

Toward the end of the Civil War a Connecticut captain with the felicitous name of Valentine laid urgent siege to a lady's heart. Lacking the time (or perhaps the money) to have his photograph taken for the cartes de visite then the rage, he substituted a sketch of himself—shown below mounted over a portion of the letter ill-treated by time. What happened to the marital hopes of the rest of the regiment, history fails to record, but Captain Valentine's suit was in vain.

> Conn. Feb. 16th. 1864.
>
> Miss Flora A. Holbrook—
>
> Let me crave your pardon in advance for the great liberty, which I am fully aware, that I, a stranger, am taking, in thus addressing you. It was sometime since, that I saw you for the first-time, myself, doubtless, unnoticed by you.
>
> I belong to the band of my Country's defenders—in this, alone, do I dare repose the trust I have, that I shall be forgiven, by one of N. England's fairest daughters.
>
> It is possible that you may have noticed in the Boston Journal several weeks since, a card, published by the reenlisted men of our Regt— the bora 5th
>
> ...if you did not,—it was to the effect, that we had reenlisted and were coming home for a 30 days furlough— That each man of us had made a _vow_ to be married _before_ _we_ _went_ _back_; and warning the girls to be ready.
>
> I have no desire that you should think more highly of me than I deserve. I will enclose my carte-de-visite, that you may judge for yourself, what manner of man I be, before taking the first step to meet the advances I am making— first, to get you interested in my behalf, then, to step in myself and make you love me.
>
> Please deal frankly with me, for 30 days is not a long time in which to form dequaintance, study each others character, and consummate a most happy event.
>
> Hoping to receive word from you soon, bidding me write again, or come myself, I will now close, w[ith] best wishes and regar[ds] you ever.
>
> Yours very r[espectfully]
> One of the [...]
>
> A letter directed to [...] Veteran..
> Rendezvous [...]
> Ca[...]
> will be duely rec[eived]
> No. I think it safer to direct si[...]
> Capt. S. T. Valentine.
> Worcester.
> Mass.